RACISM
in
AMERICAN
Stage And Screen

OLIVIA DEMBERG; W.D. PALMER

authorHOUSE

AuthorHouse™
1663 Liberty Drive
Bloomington, IN 47403
www.authorhouse.com
Phone: 833-262-8899

Published by AuthorHouse   08/19/2021

ISBN: 978-1-6655-2938-9 (sc)
ISBN: 978-1-6655-2939-6 (e)

Written by Olivia Demberg
for the Palmer Foundation as directed by W.D. Palmer

Walter D. Palmer Leadership School

Currently W. D. Palmer is the founder and director of the W. D. Palmer Foundation (est. 1955), a repository of information-gathering on racism in health, education, employment, housing, courts, prisons, higher education, military, government, politics, law, banking, insurance, etc.

He is also the founder of the Black People's University of Philadelphia (1955) Freedom School, which was the grassroots organizing and training center for grassroots community and political leadership in Philadelphia and nationally. These organizations were run as nonprofit unincorporated associations from 1955 until 1980, when the Palmer Foundation received its 501(c)(3) federal tax exemption status.

W. D. Palmer has also been a professor, teaching American Racism at the University of Pennsylvania since the 1960's and today he is a member of the Presidents Commission on 1619, the 400-year anniversary of African slavery in America.

Professor Palmer has been a social activist leading the fight against racial injustice for over seventy years in Philadelphia and around the nation. In 2018, Philadelphia honored him for the organizing work he did to reform the Philadelphia school system in 1967.

In 2020, Philadelphia honored him for 65 years of fighting for social justice throughout the country. In 1980, he led the fight for parental school choice which helped the Governor of Pennsylvania get a law passed in 1997, and in 2000 he created the Walter D. Palmer Leadership Charter School.

In 2005, he borrowed eleven million dollars to build a 55 thousand square-foot two story building on two acres of land in North Philadelphia, which was donated to the school by the City of Philadelphia, and because of the school's rapid growth, in 2010 he acquired the Saint Bartholomew Catholic High School, for his middle and high school.

In ten years, the school grew from three hundred elementary and middle school students, to two hundred preschoolers and over a thousand kindergarten to twelfth graders. In 2005,

W. D. Palmer commissioned a muralist to paint over four hundred pre-selected portraits on the school walls, corridors, and stairwells, with a goal to paint thirty fifteen foot murals in the gymnatorium.

Although the Walter D. Palmer Leadership School recruited "at risk children" that were from seventeen of the poorest zip codes in Philadelphia and 300 percent below poverty, the school boasted of a 95% daily attendance, 100% high school graduation, and 100% post graduate placement in four year and two year colleges, trade and technology schools, or military, until the school's closing in 2015.

W. D. Palmer Foundation Hashtags

1. #racedialogueusa
2. #racismdialogueusa
3. #atriskchildrenusa
4. #youthorganizingusa
5. #stopblackonblackusa
6. #newleadershipusa
7. #1619commemorationusa
8. #africanslaveryusa
9. #indigenouspeopleusa
10. #afrocentricusa
11. #civillibertiesusa
12. #civilrightsusa
13. #humanrightsusa
14. #saveourchildrenusa
15. #parentalschoolchoiceusa
16. #wearyourmaskusa
17. #defeatcovid19usa
18. #socialdistanceusa

Acknowledgement

I would like to take this time to acknowledge from the beginning of the Palmer Foundation, 1955, the many contributors who helped to gather information, organize, and write the leadership, self-development, and social awareness curriculums.

From the Palmer Foundation's inception, these contributors have been composed of community members, elementary, middle- and high-school students, as well as college student volunteers and interns, along with professional contributors.

We chose this method and process because it was consistent with our history, vision, philosophy, mission, and goals of always developing leadership in practice.

These groups, who have helped to produce our materials, are the same cohorts who over the years have helped to teach and train others as well as helped to develop a national database through which these curriculum and training materials can be distributed.

The story of the Palmer Foundation is the story of building community and leadership at the same time, and the Palmer Foundation wants to give an enthusiastic endorsement in recognition of the thousands of people who have been with us on this long and arduous journey.

We want to take this time to thank the many community leaders and people that have invited us into their communities to help them reclaim and restore the many values, properties, and people who may have been threatened with the loss of finance, property, and life, because they are the true heroes and heroines that made the Palmer Foundation the success that it has become.

Public Appeal

The Palmer Foundation is a federal 501(c)(3) organization that has spent over 65 years educating and fighting for social justice in the most underserved "at risk" communities around the country. Our goals have always been to use education for human liberation and encourage "at risk" families and children to help gather, write, produce, publish, and teach others in a similar situation.

Our mission is to disseminate our leadership, self-development, social justice, and grassroots-organizing books, manuals, and learning materials across America and around the world.

Our goals are to sell these publications or to offer them in exchange for a suggested tax-exempt donation that would allow us to continue producing our leadership training, as well as grassroots community and political organizing efforts.

Ultimately, we would like to create a satellite school as a model or prototype of the Walter D. Palmer Leadership School that could be replicated around the world, and we appeal for your enthusiastic and sustained support going forward.

Author Biography

Olivia Demberg has spent half her life in the urban metropolis of Los Angeles and half in the smaller environs of Fort Collins, Colorado. To her, both have their charms, but she considers herself more suited to the pace of a big city. Currently, she resides in Philadelphia where she has just received a Bachelor of Arts degree in Theatre Arts from the University of Pennsylvania and hopes to move to the Big Apple as theatre reopens post-pandemic. She has interned at Primary Stages in New York. When she is not researching and writing, she can be found raising service dogs for the disabled, attending any theatre production she is able, dancing a mean Lindy Hop, and napping to recover from the above.

Contents

Preface

For more than a hundred years, the entertainment industry has both struggled with and perpetuated the spectre of racism. At times, it has been guilty of portraying racist tropes or presenting employment barriers with little regard for how they extend the prejudices of society. In better moments, it has been in the forefront of breaking down barriers within society in an entertaining, thought-provoking, and pioneering way. So many of the impressions that we form come from the entertainment we consume. It is from the entertainment arts and media of each era that we learn about the prevailing attitudes toward racial minorities; it is also by way of the entertainment arts and media that we are able to educate and attempt to overturn these prejudices in the fight toward racial equality, openness, and inclusivity. Minority voices are still critically underrepresented in the world of mainstream media and entertainment. An open tent and positive portrayals of minorities in entertainment are vital to this fight.

Racism spreads like a virus with strains that develop and mutate throughout time, infecting everything that they come in contact with. Just as we have been continuously tested for coronavirus over the past year, we must check our biases regularly and be ready to correct any flaws we see in our journey toward eradicating the scourge of racism once and for all. Despite the progress that has been made, there is still a long way to go.

This book will share the research I have compiled for the Palmer Foundation on how race is portrayed historically in film and theatre, presenting examples of the successes and shortcomings that entertainment has added to the dialogue about race over the decades.

THEATRE

Musical Theatre

Shuffle Along

Aside from being one of the earliest clear precursors to the modern American musical, a show entitled *Shuffle Along* has the distinction of being one of the few musicals with an all-Black writing team and cast. Noble Sissle (composer/lyricist), Eubie Blake (composer/lyricist), Flournoy Miller (playwright), and Aubrey Lyleshas (playwright) met at a NAACP benefit in Philadelphia, Pennsylvania. Each of them was a Vaudeville veteran with no Broadway or musical writing experience. At first, promoters were skeptical that a Black-written and produced show would have widespread appeal to Broadway audiences. However, the team produced a hit sensation that would go on to be revived on Broadway four times.

The plot of *Shuffle Along* has often been described as a thin storyline mimicking that of a revue. In the show, two crooked grocery store owners, Sam and Steve, both run for mayor of Jimtown, USA with the agreement that the loser will get appointed chief of police. Aided by a dishonest campaign manager, Sam wins and keeps his promise to Steve, but they begin to butt heads, eventually resolving their differences in a comic fight. As they are fighting, the virtuous Harry Walton, their opponent in the mayoral race, promises to put an end to their corruption. He rallies the people, wins the next election, gets the girl, and runs Sam and Steve out of town.

Even though the show was a critical success, it did not always paint a favorable picture of the Black community. Much of the comedy within the show relied on old tropes and stereotypes drawn directly from the tradition of minstrelsy. One character in the show even remarked that an African-American woman is more desirable if her skin is lighter. Though much of the show urged race relations toward a step in the right direction, clearly they still had a long way to go.

The original production of *Shuffle Along* opened in 1921 and played 504 performances, a number which was unheard of at the time. Because of the roaring success of the original production, producers attempted to mount revivals of *Shuffle Along* twice only to have the productions close within weeks. However, its third revival in 2016 came at it from a completely new perspective. The revival, entitled *Shuffle Along, or, the Making of the*

Musical Sensation of 1921 and All That Followed, focused on the difficulties that the production team faced when mounting the original production of *Shuffle Along* as well as the critical acclaim it achieved and what that meant in terms of race relations in theatre and on Broadway in particular. The show featured a star-studded cast with Audra McDonald as Lottie Gee, Billy Porter as Lyles, Brian Stokes Mitchell as Miller, Joshua Henry as Sissle, and Brandon Victor Dixon as Blake. It was received with mostly positive critical acclaim, especially noting the standout performance by Audra McDonald. In his review for *The Wall Street Journal*, Terry Teachout wrote, "The cast, led by Audra McDonald, Brian Stokes Mitchell and Billy Porter, is as charismatic as you'd expect, and Savion Glover's near-nonstop choreography explodes off the stage with the unrelenting impact of a flamethrower. But then comes intermission, and what had looked like a masterpiece goes flat and stays that way." [1]

In spite of all of its flaws, the success of *Shuffle Along* marked a massive breakthrough for Black performers in the 1920s and proved to producers the marketability of African-American talent on Broadway. The original production of *Shuffle Along* was embraced wholeheartedly by the African-American community because it was "one of the first shows to provide the right mixture of primitivism and satire, enticement and respectability, blackface humor and romance, to satisfy its customers." [2] Its success ushered in a new attitude of acceptance and respect for African-American musicals on Broadway, which included the portrayal of a sophisticated love story for African-Americans, instead of resorting to the trope of comedic ones as had been done in the past.

However, the critical success of the show did have its drawbacks. "Any show that followed the characteristics of Shuffle Along could usually be assured of favorable reviews or at the very least a modest audience response. Yet, if a show strayed from what had become the standard formula for the Black musical, disastrous reviews became almost inevitable... The result of this critical stranglehold on the Black musical was that... Black authors and composers prepared shows within extremely narrow constraints." [3] Thus, the breakout success of the show presented a new set of constraints to combat in Black American Musical Theatre.

---

[1] Terry Teachout, "Shuffle Along Review: Half of Perfection" in *The Wall Street Journal*, (New York: April 28, 2016).

[2] David Krasner, "A Beautiful Pageant: African American Theatre" in *Drama and Performance in the Harlem Renaissance, 1910-1927*, (London: 2002), pp. 263–67.

[3] Allen Woll, *Black Musicals: From Coontown to Dreamgirls* (Boston, MA: Da Capo Press, 1989), p. 78.

Show Boat

Based on Edna Ferber's best-selling 1926 novel of the same name with music by Jerome Kern, lyrics by Oscar Hammerstein II and P. G. Wodehouse, and a book also by Oscar Hammerstein II, *Show Boat* follows the lives of the performers, stagehands and dock workers on a Mississippi River show boat over the course of 40 years. Set approximately a decade after the end of the Reconstruction era when the South was rife with Jim Crow laws that legalized racial segregation, the show brings to the forefront impactful and relevant themes such as racial prejudice and tragic love.

Show Boat opened on Broadway at the Ziegfeld Theatre on December 27, 1927 to rave reviews. In his review for the New York Times, Brooks Atkinson hailed the adaptation of the book as "intelligently made" and the production one of "unimpeachable skill and taste." [4] Although originally written for Paul Robeson who was unavailable for the debut of the show, Brooks Atkinson did get a chance to see him in the role tailored for him, writing "Mr. Robeson has a touch of genius. It is not merely his voice, which is one of the richest organs on the stage. It is his understanding that gives 'Old Man River' an epic lift. When he sings...you realize that Jerome Kern's spiritual has reached its final expression." [5] *Show Boat* played 572 performances before it closed in 1929, which was considered a remarkably long run at the time.

Even though it was initially received incredibly well, the language and treatment of Black characters in the show quickly became outdated, resulting in the show having to be rewritten multiple times to be more in-sync with the current social climate of the era of each revival. One of the most glaring issues with the show was the way in which it normalized the use of the N word. In addition, much of the dialogue and lyrics of the Black characters is written in what is known as African American Vernacular English. Whether or not the original writers thought that this language was an accurate reflection of the speech patterns of black people in Mississippi at the time, its use within the show and beyond only serves to perpetuate racial stereotypes.

In 1993, legendary theatre producer Harold Prince mounted a revival of *Show Boat*. Due to the outdated nature of many of the stereotypical viewpoints in the original production, this could have gone horribly awry in the wrong hands and reinforced racist tropes that had more or less died out in the intervening years. However, instead of trying to bury the

---

[4] J. Brooks Atkinson, "Show Boat" in *The New York Times* (New York: 1927).

[5] J. Brooks Atkinson, "THE PLAY; Show Boat" as Good as New" in *The New York Times* (New York: 1932).

show's racist roots, Prince used the story (with necessary changes, of course) to highlight the inequities of the topics within it. As stated by prominent columnist, critic, and arts and entertainment editor Jeremy Gerard,

> Hammerstein eventually changed the lyric to "colored folk," which Prince retains. But he purposefully keeps the word "nigger" in the dialogue… Indeed, rather than mute the show's racial and class distinctions, Prince and Lee have set them in high relief without ever undermining one of the most beautiful scores ever written.[6]

Aside from having the distinction of being the production that theatre great Paul Robeson is best known for, *Show Boat* was a musical that was daringly liberal for its time. It broke countless barriers - it was the first racially-integrated musical in which Black and white people performed together on the same stage, it was the first Broadway musical to feature an interracial marriage, and it was one of the first shows to adopt a tone of sympathy rather than condescension toward the Black community. This was a massive step forward for representation of Black people in theatre, but theatre still had a long way to go before it could free itself from its biases and represent the Black community in the way it deserved.

Finian's Rainbow

With a book by E.Y. Harburg and Fred Saidy, lyrics by Harburg, and music by Burton Lane, the show notably served as one of the first attempts by American theatre to challenge racism and bigotry.

Finians's Rainbow tells the story of an elderly Irishman who moves to the southern United States with his daughter Sharon with the intent of burying a stolen pot of gold near Fort Knox, mistakenly believing that it will grow. Og, the leprechaun to whom the pot of gold belongs, follows them in a desperate attempt to recover it before the loss of it turns him permanently human. However, a wrench is thrown into things when a crooked, bigoted U.S. Senator gets involved, and road blocks arise when wishes are made unintentionally over the hidden pot of gold.

---

[6] Jeremy Gerard, "Show Boat" in *Variety* (Los Angeles, CA: 1994).

The original production of *Finian's Rainbow* opened on Broadway on January 10, 1947 at the 46th Street Theatre and ran for 725 performances. A film version of the much beloved classic was released in 1968 and several revivals have followed. Due to its magic and whimsy, the show quickly became a beloved classic. However, major revivals of the show have become increasingly rare over time because of its dated treatment of racism in the American South.

Despite its landmark status as Broadway's first fully integrated production, the show has a number of issues. One of the most prominent issues is that there are only two fully-fleshed out roles for Black actors - a little boy named Henry and a Tuskegee University student named Howard. According to Russel Peterson's article "I Was a Teenage Negro! Blackface as a Vehicle of White Liberalism in Finian's Rainbow," the role of Henry is "by far the most developed children's role, which may have been a calculatedly 'progressive' gesture on the part of Harburg and Saidy. In spite of this, however, Henry's character is defined strictly within the bounds of "positive" essentialism." [7] Peterson is noting that Henry's characteristics that make him smart and crucial to the plot are stereotyped essences generally associated with the Black community, and these traits are used in service of a white character. While the white writers consider the traits positive, they are still racist tropes. As for the character of Howard, although he only appears in one scene, he manages to make a big impression on the audience. Peterson says,

> Howard is the very model of the New Negro: intelligent, educated, and dignified... In its direct refutation of negative stereotypes, and its overt critique of "Gone With the Wind"-style representations of African Americans, this scene is arguably Finian's satirical highpoint... Howard turns the demeaning stereotype into an instrument of comeuppance for the white bigot, in what could justly be described as an act of "signifying." [8]

Finian's Rainbow presents a bold departure from the tradition of minstrelsy with its brave and brazen assault on Jim Crow laws of the American South at the time. However, it also presents the implication that racial tolerance can only be achieved through literal magic. Peterson puts it well when he says, "Finian's simplistically progressive fable of

---

[7] Russel Peterson, "I Was a Teenage Negro! Blackface as a Vehicle of White Liberalism in Finian's Rainbow," in *American Studies*, Vol. 47, No. ¾ (Kansas: 2006).

[8] Ibid.

racial tolerance presents, upon closer inspection, a picture of progressive intentions and regressive assumptions that is far from Black and white." [9]

West Side Story

Another musical that has been influential in the dialogue concerning racial tension in America is *West Side Story*. Although the original production did not address the experience of discrimination amoong Black Americans, racial tension is one of the most prominent themes in the show, and the changes made in the most recent revival incorporate the experiences of the Black community into that dialogue.

The original production of *West Side Story* premiered on Broadway in 1957 and was met with widespread audience and mostly positive critical acclaim. Inspired by Shakespeare's Romeo & Juliet, West Side Story follows the lives and interactions of two rival gangs on the Upper West Side of New York City - the Jets and the Sharks. The Jets, as portrayed in the original, are Caucasians of European descent - immigrants at one time, but ones that feel they planted their flag first and therefore have legitimacy of turf ownership - while the Sharks are recent Hispanic immigrants from Puerto Rico. The story follows Tony, a former member of the Jets, who falls in love with Maria, the younger sister of Bernardo, leader of the Sharks.

From its edgy choreography by Jerome Robbins to its book by Arthur Laurents and score with music and lyrics by Leonard Bernstein and Stephen Sondheim respectively, everything about it was a roaring audience pleaser. The show was lauded as a bold departure from the theatre that had come before it. Among the rave reviews it received, John Chapman praised the show's "lovely and moving" plot, its "fascinatingly tricky and melodically beguiling" score with lyrics that "have [a] simple grace," and its choreography that "[carries] the plot as much as the spoken words and lyrics do." [10] He even praises the cast of "young people of whom few have been heard" who "dance and act with such skill and sincerity that they bring the audience out of its seats and up on the stage with them." [11]

---

[9] Ibid.

[10] John Chapman, "*West Side Story*, a Splendid and Super-Modern Musical Drama" in *New York Daily News*, (New York: 1957).

[11] Ibid.

Since its debut, West Side Story has become a beloved classic that has been produced countless times - high school productions, multiple national tours, a West End transfer and subsequent revivals, and multiple Broadway revivals, all faithful to the original in virtually every way - until now. Therefore, it is a brave director who takes on the daunting challenge of modernizing it. Ivo van Hove, a Belgian theatre director who is well-known for his avant-garde theatre productions, undertook the task with his revival opening briefly on Broadway on February 20, 2020 and then shuttering due to the COVID-19 pandemic.

Van Hove's "West Side Story for the 21st century" [12] is the first departure from the original, and it is most definitely modern. A mixed-media spectacle, it was conceived with the goal of portraying "the America of today" and placing a spotlight on "the raw energy that's hidden within West Side Story." [13] As van Hove states in an interview, "It's the sociological story, the political dimension of the story that interests me most." [14] With those ideas in mind, van Hove made a number of changes and cuts that have sparked much controversy.

Ivo van Hove modernized the production in several ways including but not limited to the addition of Black Jets and the use of cell phones as recording devices whenever there is a threat of police violence. In one instance, an episode of harassment by Officer Krupke is deescalated when one of the gang members begins to film it. This threat of exposure stops Krupke right in his tracks. In another instance, a technique of broadening our viewpoint with documentary style images as background turns the song, Gee, Officer Krupke, from comic relief into a chilling reminder of the marginalization of these characters by institutions like the police and the prison industrial complex. Shots of the police arresting young men, interrogating them, and imprisoning them are juxtaposed with the foreground action of the Jets down on their knees with their hands behind their heads - a direct correlation with "hands up, don't shoot" from the Black Lives Matter movement. Although *West Side Story* began as a story rooted in the experiences of the hispanic community with racism, its message is clearly a universal one.

---

[12] Alexis Soloski, "'The violence should be tangible' – Ivo van Hove on roughing up *West Side Story*" in *The Guardian*, (New York: 2020).

[13] Ibid.

[14] Daniel Pollack-Pelzner, "Why *West Side Story* Abandoned Its Queer Narrative" in *The Atlantic*, (New York: 2020).

The Wiz

With music and lyrics by Charlie Smalls (as well as smaller contributions by others) and a book by William F. Brown, *The Wiz* is a retelling of the well-known and beloved children's novel *The Wonderful Wizard of Oz* written by L. Frank Baum in 1900. However, *The Wiz* is distinct from *The Wonderful Wizard of Oz* because the original story has been reframed by the contemporary African-American culture of the time. *The Wiz* premiered in Baltimore at the Morris A. Mechanic Theatre on October 21, 1974. It played there until 1975, when it opened on Broadway at the Majestic Theatre on January 5. There, it received great critical acclaim and went on to win seven Tony Awards, including the Tony Award for Best Musical. The original production of *The Wiz* ran for 1,672 performances and closed on January 28, 1979.

As *The Wiz* grew in popularity, countless productions and revivals of the show have been staged all over the world. In 1978, it was adapted into a film, in which Ted Ross and Mabel King reprised their roles from the Broadway production as the Cowardly Lion and Evillene respectively. Sadly, the film was a critical and commercial failure due to the casting of a too old for the part Diana Ross as Dorothy. Despite its chilly reception, the film was considered important because the Black community was seeing itself reflected on screen in a way they never had before. As Gerrick D. Kennedy said in his article for the *LA Times* entitled "On its 40th anniversary, a look at how 'The Wiz' forever changed black culture," "For a generation of black Americans, this was the first time they saw people who spoke, sung (sic) and moved the way they did in a Broadway production and, later, a big-screen musical, and it has become a kind of rite of passage for the black community." [15] Decades later, NBC produced *The Wiz Live!* as a television special on December 3, 2015 with an encore performance only sixteen days later.

The Wiz played an important role in facilitating Broadway's mainstream acceptance of works with an all-Black cast. The show explored themes such as slavery, emancipation, the great migration, and faith. The dance numbers incorporated traditional movement from the African diaspora along with ballet, jazz and modern movement that has become closely associated with Black dance.

The Wiz even had the distinction of being the first Black musical that was said to be "entirely post-Jim Crow" in the sense that, while the cast may have been all Black and they

---

[15] Gerrick D. Kennedy, "On its 40th anniversary, a look at how 'The Wiz' forever changed black culture" in *Los Angeles Times*, (Los Angeles, CA: 2018).

were telling a story of racial liberation, none of the actors was portraying a slave. *The Wiz* told a story of the perseverance of the Black American dream despite mighty odds in a way that no other work had done before.

Hello, Dolly!

Hello, Dolly! is a Golden Age musical with lyrics and music by Jerry Herman and a book by Michael Stewart. Based on Thornton Wilder's 1938 farce *The Merchant of Yonkers*, *Hello, Dolly!* tells the story of Dolly Gallagher Levi, a matchmaker with an iron will, as she journeys to Yonkers, New York, to set up Horace Vandergelder, a miserly "well-known unmarried half-a-millionaire," with a match. The musical premiered in Detroit at the Fisher Theatre on November 18, 1963 and played there until it moved to Broadway, opening at the St. James Theatre on January 16, 1964.

There, it received rave reviews from critics and audience members alike and went on to sweep the Tony Awards, winning awards in ten out of the eleven categories in which it was nominated including the Tony Award for Best Musical. The original production of *Hello, Dolly!* ran for 2,844 performances and closed on December 27, 1970. Although the original production of the show was unremarkable in terms of diverse casting, the all-Black cast of the 1975 revival of *Hello, Dolly!* at the Minskoff Theatre proved that the popularity of Golden Age musicals is not dependent upon them being performed under the same racialized casting conditions as the original productions.

Dreamgirls

With music by Henry Krieger and lyrics and a book by Tom Eyen, the beloved musical *Dreamgirls* follows the rise to fame of "The Dreams," a fictional female vocal trio from Chicago, Illinois. The story is loosely based on the show business aspirations and successes of various rhythm and blues acts such as Martha & The Vandellas and The Supremes that were characterized by the Motown sound. *Dreamgirls* premiered on Broadway at the Imperial Theatre on December 20, 1981. In spite of Diana Ross' criticism of it for what she saw as an appropriation of her life story, it opened to mostly positive critical reviews and received multiple Tony Award nominations. The production ran for 1,521 performances and closed on August 11, 1985. The musical was eventually adapted into a film by DreamWorks and Paramount Pictures in 2006.

Many of the songs from *Dreamgirls* share the common theme of race because it was a central issue in the '60's, the era in which the musical is set. Although the show does bring to the forefront a story of Black women in entertainment and addresses racism front and center, the fact that the show had a mostly white writing team still underscores the ongoing neglect of Black creators in the world of musical theatre.

Once on this Island

With a book and lyrics by Lynn Ahrens and music by Stephen Flaherty, *Once on this Island* tells the story of a peasant girl on an island in the Caribbean who brings two vastly different groups of people together using the power of love. *Once on this Island* premiered Off-Broadway at Playwrights Horizons in May of 1990. The subsequent Broadway production opened at the Booth Theatre on October 18, 1990, featuring LaChanze as Ti Moune and Jerry Dixon as Daniel. The show was well-received, being praised for its honest and concise dialogue and for having "the integrity of genuine fairy tales, in that it doesn't lead to a saccharine ending but to a catharsis." [16] The original production closed on December 1, 1991 after running for a total of 488 performances.

The show is set on an island in the French Antilles archipelago and begins as a storm is quickly approaching. The thunder of the impending storm scares a young girl, so, in an attempt to comfort her, the villagers tell her the story of Ti Moune, a peasant girl who falls in love with Daniel Beauxhomme, who is what the villagers call "a grand homme," meaning that he is from the wealthy, elite side of the island. They tell of four gods who rule over an island called the Jewel of the Antilles - Asaka, Mother of the Earth, Agwé, god of Water, Erzulie, goddess of Love, and Papa Ge, demon of Death. The peasants on the island worship them and pray to them for the fulfillment of all their needs. In one song, the peasants are described as "black as night" and they live on one side of the island, while the *grand hommes* - the lighter-skinned descendants of the original French planters that immigrated there - live on the other. This difference in skin tone - a relative lightness or darkness - serves as the basis for the rift between the two groups, which is a phenomenon

---

[16] Frank Rich, "'Once on This Island,' Fairy Tale Bringing Caribbean to 42ⁿᵈ Street" in *The New York Times*, (New York: 1990).

that is widely known as colorism. In an article entitled "Once on This Island," journalist Jason Lee discusses the issues of race and class in communities of color," He writes that "Colorism within the black community goes back to slavery when darker skinned slaves worked the fields while the lighter skinned slaves worked inside their owner's homes. This separated classes even among the race and is an important part of history that plays out among [the Black community] and other people of color." [17] The importance here is in acknowledging that racism is not merely a prejudice of one race towards another but occurs within a race towards its own members. It challenges the audience to examine intra-racial prejudice. Thus, the message of the play is to love with no regard for superficial constraints such as complexion.

Ragtime

Based on the 1975 novel of the same name by E.L. Doctorow with music composed by Stephen Flaherty, lyrics written by Lynn Ahrens, and a book written by Terrence McNally, *Ragtime* tells the story of three unique demographics - African Americans, upper-class white suburbanites, and Eastern European immigrants - in the United States in the early 20th century. Each group, or social caste, is represented by a central character and his or her family that supposedly embodies the quintessential characteristics of that demographic. African Americans are represented by Coalhouse Walker Jr., a Harlem musician, and his love interest, Sarah. The upper-class suburbanites are represented by the character of Mother and her family, an upper-class white family in New Rochelle, New York. The Eastern European immigrants are represented by Tateh and his young daughter, Jewish immigrants from Latvia. The story is narrated by such luminaries as J.P. Morgan, Harry Houdini, Henry Ford, Emma Goldman, Booker T. Washington, and Evelyn Nesbit, and their narration works to connect the three worlds in the play.

Ragtime premiered in Toronto in December 1996 and in the US at the Shubert Theatre in Los Angeles in June 1997. The show opened on Broadway on January 18, 1998 at the Ford Center for the Performing Arts. The original cast included big names such as Brian Stokes Mitchell, Marin Mazzie, and Audra McDonald. The production opened to mixed reviews in which many critics pointed out issues in the script that were masked

---

[17] Jasen Lee, "'Once on This Island' discusses issues of race and class in communities of color" in *Deseret News*, (Utah: 2020).

by the opulence of the production design that included fireworks and a working Model T automobile. In his review for *The New York Times*, Ben Brantley calls the show "a spectacular feast for the eyes," but states it also has "the aura of something assembled by corporate committee… The skills and virtues of *Ragtime*… are many and undeniable; but a distinctive human personality is not among them." [18] Writing for *Variety*, Greg Evans seems to agree, describing the show as "a musical easier to admire than love," calling the second act "both overwrought and dull." [19] The show closed on January 16, 2000 after 861 performances.

Although *Ragtime* is regarded as "a crowning work of theater for the millennium" [20] by a number of critics, it had a primarily white writing team, which only perpetuates the ongoing neglect of Black voices in theatre

---

Hairspray

Based on a 1988 film of the same name with music and lyrics written by Marc Shaiman and Scott Wittman and a book by Mark O'Donnell and Thomas Meehan, *Hairspray* tells the story of Tracy Turnblad, a teenager in the 1960s from Baltimore, Maryland whose dream is to dance on *The Corny Collins Show*, but is discouraged from auditioning for fear that she would be ridiculed for her weight. Ultimately, her fear of this prejudice comes true when she is rejected from the show, along with a young Black girl named Little Inez. The injustice of both of these prejudices frustrates Tracy. At school, Tracy finds herself in detention for "inappropriate hair height" along with a Black dancer named Seaweed who teaches her some new moves that land her a spot on the show despite her weight. Tracy becomes a hit, and she uses her newfound star status as a platform to advocate for racial integration on television.

The original production of *Hairspray* opened on Broadway at the Neil Simon Theatre on August 15, 2002 after a successful tryout in Seattle earlier that same year. At the 2003 Tony Awards, the show won eight awards, including one for Best Musical. Although the show received mostly favorable reviews, there were a handful of mixed ones. Ben Brantley stated

---

[18] Ben Brantley, "Theater Review; 'Ragtime': A Diorama With Nostalgia Rampant" in *The New York Times*, (New York: 1998).

[19] Greg Evans, "Ragtime" in *Variety*, (Los Angeles, CA: 1998).

[20] Richard Christiansen, "A Great Show When it Premiered, 'Ragtime' Gets Even Better in Chicago" in *Chicago Tribune*, (Chicago: 1998).

in his article for *The New York Times* that the show "succeeds in recreating the pleasures of the old-fashioned musical comedy without seeming old-fashioned." [21] However, he also pointed out that there were rare moments where the comedic stylings became repetitive and noted that the show "overdoes the self-help-style anthems of uplift." [22] *Hairspray* went on to run for 2,642 performances and closed on January 4, 2009. Multiple productions of *Hairspray* went on to open internationally in London with a subsequent revival, in Australia, and more. To date, the show has completed one US tour and four UK tours. The musical gained so much popularity that NBC decided to produce *Hairspray Live!* as a television special event in 2016.

One of the primary themes at the forefront of *Hairspray* is the issue of racism. Set in the 1960s, the musical highlights the prevalence of racial discrimination against African-Americans during the The Civil Rights Movement (1954-1986). Although this is viewed in retrospect as a positive time in America's history because of the progress it achieved in allowing African-Americans the right to vote, the Black community still faced the reality of white people having a monopoly over all institutional and political power. *The Corny Collins Show* is all-white with African-Americans only being permitted to dance on the show once a month in addition to being presented with a stereotypical racial representation of dance style that is parallel to the reality of the 1960s. By the end of the show however, due in large part to Tracy's efforts, the show becomes racially integrated.

Although it was written after the airing of NBC's *Hairspray Live!* rather than for the Broadway production, Matthew Delmont's article for *The Atlantic* entitled "Hairspray's Revealing Portrayal of Racism in America" sums it up well. While he praises the show for making the harsh reality of a country's history accessible and intriguing for each and every audience member, he also points out that it offers a rather simplistic solution to the deeply rooted issue of racism in the United States. He criticizes "the story's feel-good conclusion [that] implies that colorblindness is the silver bullet that ends racial discrimination, that good intentions and individual acts of bravery are enough to bring about harmony," [23] which is well-intentioned but naive. He also makes the important point that,

> It suggests a way of understanding race that allows viewers to disavow bigotry—framed in the story as the belief that white and black Americans

---

[21] Ben Brantley, "Through Hot Pink Glasses, a World That's Nice" in *The New York Times*, (New York: 2002).

[22] Ibid.

[23] M. Delmont, "'Hairspray' Is a Revealing Portrayal of Racism in America," in *The Atlantic*, (Washington, D.C.: 2017).

should live in separate spheres—without acknowledging, confronting, or seeking to overturn the actual structures of discrimination. This sort of nearsighted, if not disingenuous, framing persists today, whether in affluent parents in New York City insisting their opposition to school rezoning proposals is not about race, or in arguments suggesting that the best way to address racism is to stop accusing people of being "racists." [24]

Racism will only cease to exist if we continue to call out people's internal biases that they might not recognize as racist. We must examine our own behaviors and biases whether intentional or not and question the systems put in place in our society to perpetuate that discrimination in order to be able to dismantle those systems.

The Color Purple

Based on the 1982 novel of the same name by Alice Walker and its 1985 film adaptation, *The Color Purple* follows the difficult life of a Black woman who lives in the American South in the early-to-mid-20th century and her journey toward finding self-love. The musical features a book by Marsha Norman and music and lyrics by Brenda Russell, Allee Willis, and Stephen Bray. Although most of the creative team for the musical is white, the cast and the author of the original book are Black.

The musical tells the story of Celie who is living in Georgia with her sister, Nettie. Celie was molested by her father from a young age, and, by the tender age of fourteen, she has had two children fathered by him, both of whom her father adopts out, though the audience is initially led to believe the children have suffered a worse fate. Celie's father then marries her off to a local widower named Mister who is looking for a wife, causing her to become estranged from Nettie. Mister is abusive and has been carrying on a long time affair with a glamorous jazz singer by the name of Shug Avery, who ends up revealing information that eventually reunites Celie with her estranged sister and her two long-lost children.

Originally workshopped by the Alliance Theatre in Atlanta, Georgia in 2004, *The Color Purple* opened on Broadway at The Broadway Theatre on December 1, 2005, starring LaChanze as Celie and featuring other celebrated names in theatre such as Brandon Victor Dixon and Renee Elise Goldsberry. The show closed on February 24, 2008 after 940

---

[24] Ibid.

performances, quickly followed by the launching of three national tours and the opening of productions of *The Color Purple* all over the world - London, South Africa, Brazil, and more. A Broadway revival of *The Color Purple* was staged in 2015, with Cynthia Erivo from the London production reprising her role as Celie and featuring Jennifer Hudson as Shug. The revival took home the 2016 Tony Award for Best Revival of a Musical and closed on January 8, 2017 after 482 performances.

The original production opened to mixed reviews, yet all highlighted the importance of such a story as *The Color Purple* in which Black women find their inner warriors while noting countless technical flaws in translating such a dense story to the stage. The Broadway revival took these notes seriously and, under the direction of John Doyle, stripped the musical down to its bare essentials. This approach "allows audiences to zero in on a show's musical and emotional essence, while seeming to place narrative control directly in the hands of the performers." [25] This effectively placed greater emphasis on the character development taking place throughout the show rather than the ancillary surroundings.

The Color Purple added a great deal to the dialogue about race in America. As a Black woman living in the pre-Civil Rights South during the days of legal segregation and Jim Crow laws, Celie has an air of defeatism surrounding her - African-Americans were frequent targets of discrimination and hate crimes, a fact that many people of the time simply accepted. However, as Celie learns about the rich cultures and civilizations present in Africa and redefines her relationship with God, she gains a great deal of pride in her heritage and thus becomes more self-assured and less accepting of the prejudices directed at her.

Hamilton

Based on the 2004 biography *Alexander Hamilton* by Ron Chernow, *Hamilton: An American Musical* portrays the life of Alexander Hamilton, one of America's Founding Fathers. For the fully sung-through score of the show, *Hamilton*'s writer, Lin-Manuel Miranda, drew his inspiration primarily from musical genres such as rap, R&B, and

---

[25] Ben Brantley, "'The Color Purple' on Broadway, Stripped to Its Essence" in *The New York Times*, (New York: 2015).

hip-hop, while also incorporating elements of jazz, 1960's British pop, and more. This resulted in a very contemporary sound unlike any that theatregoers had previously experienced.

Immediately following its Off-Broadway premiere at the Public Theater on January 20, 2015, the show received great critical acclaim and sold out its twice-extended, nearly five-month long run at the Public. After winning eight Drama Desk Awards including Outstanding Musical, *Hamilton* transferred to the Richard Rodgers Theatre and opened on Broadway on August 6, 2015, once again to rave reviews. In her article in *The New Yorker*, Rebecca Mead called the show "an achievement of historical and cultural reimagining," [26] while the Pulitzer committee deemed it a "landmark American musical." These rave reviews resulted in record high box office sales and astronomical ticket prices that made it impossible to get tickets for years except by connections in high places or through the show's lottery system.

At the 2016 Tony Awards, *Hamilton* received a record-breaking 16 nominations and won 11 awards, including Best Musical. It fell just short of breaking the record for most Tony awards won by one musical, a record of 12 held by *The Producers*. That year, it also won the Grammy for Best Musical Theatre Album as well as the Pulitzer Prize for Drama. *Hamilton* has gone on to become a worldwide phenomenon, opening a production on the West End in 2017 and launching multiple separate North American tours.

Aside from its pioneering role in the world of modern musical theatre, Hamilton broke boundaries with its leading principle of "color-conscious" casting. Although the Founding Fathers of the United States were primarily white, Miranda chose to cast Black, Latino and Asian actors to play the majority of these roles in an effort to modernize the story. Miranda says, "Our cast looks like America looks now, and that's certainly intentional." [27] He also noted that, "We're telling the story of old, dead white men but we're using actors of color, and that makes the story more immediate and more accessible to a contemporary audience." [28] In addition to the added relevance, the casting of Black, Latino, and Asian American leads allows audiences to view America as it originally was - a nation of immigrants - which effectively rendered the whiteness of the Founding Fathers irrelevant to their claim on the country. Also at the forefront of *Hamilton* is the show's

---

[26] Rebecca Mead, "All About the Hamiltons" in *The New Yorker*, (New York: 2015).

[27] M. Paulsen, "'Hamilton' Heads to Broadway in a Hip-Hop Retelling" in *The New York Times*. (New York: 2015).

[28] Frank DiGiacomo, "'Hamilton's' Lin-Manuel Miranda on Finding Originality, Racial Politics (and Why Trump Should See His Show)" in *The Hollywood Reporter*, Los Angeles, CA: 2015).

pro-immigration stance, as it shifts focus from his whiteness and highlights the status of Alexander Hamilton as an immigrant, with lyrics that work to foster a positive image of immigrants, such as "immigrants, we get the job done."

Although the casting of Black and Latino actors to play white historical figures has drawn an inundation of praise from many, some have condemned this choice as Black people celebrating the white men who had once enslaved them. Scholars have attempted to combat this narrative by arguing that *Hamilton* serves as a vehicle for educating people about the real history of the nation. It is only by remembering and discussing the downfalls alongside the positive aspects of a country's beginning that we can ensure that we avoid making those same mistakes in the future.

A Strange Loop

A Strange Loop is based on the life story of its writer, a gay, Black man by the name of Michael R. Jackson, and tells the story of a gay, Black man named Usher, who coincidentally works a day job as an usher at a Broadway theatre. Usher aspires to be a successful musical theatre writer but is met with a great deal of backlash from the white, heteronormative world in which he lives. He is in the process of ghost writing a new Tyler Perry musical, but his passion project is actually a musical he is writing about a gay, Black man who is trying to write a musical about a gay, Black man who is trying to write a musical about a gay, Black man who is trying to write a musical, and so on. The show features a seven-person cast, consisting of Usher and six ensemble members who voice his thoughts as well as play various characters throughout the show. Each cast member in the show is Black and queer.

The show premiered Off-Broadway at Playwrights Horizons and ran from May 24 to July 28, 2019 with every single performance sold out. It received rave reviews from countless critics. Elysa Gardener wrote for the *New York Stage Review* that "Much of the show is sung, with whip smart dialogue rushing into lyrics dense with au courant terms and references and wordplay, much of it concerning race, gender and sexual identity, some of it too raw to be reproduced here." [29] Philip Boroff of the *Broadway Journal* described the show as "funny, raunchy and painfully honest" and even theorized that "With some developmental work, one can imagine A Strange Loop expanding boundaries on Broadway." [30]

---

[29] Elysa Gardner, "A Strange Loop: The Cycle of Life, On Repeat" in *New York Stage Review*, (New York: 2019).

[30] Philip Boroff, "'A Strange Loop' Expands Boundaries: Review" in *Broadway Journal*, (New York: 2019).

On May 4, 2020, Michael R. Jackson made history when he was awarded the Pulitzer Prize for Drama for *A Strange Loop* with the committee describing the show as "A metafictional musical that tracks the creative process of an artist transforming issues of identity, race, and sexuality that once pushed him to the margins of the cultural mainstream into a meditation on universal human fears and insecurities." [31] With that, the show became the tenth musical to win the Pulitzer Prize for Drama and holds the distinction of being the first musical written by a Black person to win the award as well as the first musical to win without a Broadway run. As Frank Rizzo says in his review for *Variety*, "both Usher's journey and Jackson's show offer bracing insights into the endless strata of conflicts faced by those who are young, gifted and black — and so much more." [32]

---

[31] "A Strange Loop, by Michael R. Jackson". The Pulitzer Prizes. Retrieved 4 May 2020.

[32] Frank Rizzo, "Off Broadway Review: 'A Strange Loop'" in *Variety*, (Los Angeles, CA: 2019).

Other Plays

1823

The Drama of King Shotaway - William Henry Brown
- First known play by a Black playwright in the United States
- Based on the life of Joseph Chatoyer, a Garifuna chief, who led a Black Carib revolt on the island of St Vincent against British rule in 1795.
- Playwright William Henry Brown founded the African theater in the 1820s

---

1829

Metamora; or, The Last of the Wampanoags - John Augustus Stone
- The play was written because of a contest hosted by Edwin Forrest with a prize of $500
- The play is set in 17th century New England around the time of the arrival of the Puritans
- The story is about English settlers and their conflict with the native Wampanoags who are initially peaceful until violence erupts.

1859

The Octoroon - Dion Boucicault
- Adapted from from the novel *The Quadroon* by Thomas Mayne Reid
- An ill-fated love story on a Louisiana plantation between a White man and an Octoroon woman who is legally a slave. It sparked debates about the abolishment of slavery as well as the role of theatre in politics
- Contains elements of Romanticism and melodrama

Osawatomie Brown - Kate Edwards
- About John Brown's attack on slave owners in Kansas and the ensuing raid on Harper's Ferry
- Premiered two weeks after Brown's execution

1909

The Nigger - Edward Sheldon

- Explores the relationship between Blacks and whites in the melodrama of a politician facing exposure of his Black lineage and the ruin that could bring
- First performed on Broadway in NYC at the New Theatre on December 4, 1909
- Adapted to a novel and a film directed by Edgar Lewis in 1915

1911

Disraeli - Louis N. Parker

- A biographical play about British Prime Minister Benjamin Disraei as he attempts to gain control of the Suez Canal to secure Britain's route to India in 1875. Disraeli contends with antisemitism.
- Commissioned by actor George Arliss in 1910
- Three film adaptations of the play. Arliss starred in the last one and won an Academy Award for his performance.

The Star of Ethiopia - W. E. B. Du Bois

- Written by leading New Negro intellectual to educate Blacks and whites
- Presented as an American historical pageant with a prologue and five scenes detailing the history of the Black man from prehistoric times, through slavery, to the climb back up
- Only four known performances but they were highly successful

1922

Loyalties - John Galsworthy

- Antisemitism comes into play between a group of friends when one accuses another of theft.
- Staged at St Martins Theatre and ran for over a year

Taboo - Mary Hoyt Wiborg

- Paul Robeson's professional debut
- Set on a plantation in Louisiana before the American Civil War and in Africa
- Starred Robeson, Margaret Wycherly (the only white member of the cast), other African American actors, and African students at Columbia University.

1924

All God's Chillun Got Wings - Eugene O'Neill

- Expressionist play by Eugene O'Neill about miscegenation inspired by the old Negro spiritual
- Arguably one of his most controversial of plays, it starred Paul Robeson in the premiere, in which he portrayed the Black husband of an abusive white woman, who, resenting her husband's skin color, destroys his promising career as a lawyer
- Culminated with Jim metaphorically consummating his marriage with his white wife by symbolically emasculating himself
- Opening was postponed due to nationwide controversy over its plot

1926

Color Struck - Zora Neale Hurston

- A woman's jealous fear of being left for a lighter-skinned woman is the cause of her failed relationship and the loss of her daughter
- A play about colorism in the Black community

In Abraham's Bosom - Paul Green

- Set in the Southeast of the United States, from 1885 to the beginning of the 20th century
- Abe McCranie is a mixed-race African American field worker who tries to start a school to educate Black children, as they are underserved by the state. Ultimately, he gets a school, but the white people run him out of it and drive him to murder.

1928

The Purple Flower - Marita Bonner

- A one-act play typically considered to be Bonner's masterpiece
- Not set in any specific place or time, it is a metaphor for racial issues in the United States
- The White Devils live on the hill where the purple flower of life grows, while the Us's who worked to build the town are forced to live in the valley below. They spend their time trying to devise ways to get up the hill, however, after two hundred years of slavery they realize they have gotten nowhere.

1929

Exit: An Illusion - Marita Bonner

- Three character play focusing on the difficulties that mixed-race women face, belonging to two (or more) races but not fully accepted by either.
- An example of surrealist drama, very unusual for the time in which the playwright lived
- Not performed in her lifetime
- one of the frequently unrecognized Black female writers of the Harlem Renaissance
- Resisted universalizing, essentialist tendencies of other Black writers by focusing on the atypical rather than the archetypal.

1930

The Green Pastures - Marc Connelly

- Adapted from *Ol' Man Adam an' His Chillun,* a collection of stories
- Portrays episodes from the Old Testament as seen through the eyes of a young African American child in the Great Depression-era Southern United States

Songs of the Harlem River: Forgotten One Acts of the Harlem Renaissance - various playwrights

- A collection of five one-act plays written between 1920 and 1930 by several African American playwrights at the time including Marita Bonner, Ralf M. Coleman, Georgia Douglas Johnson, Willis Richardson, and Eulalie Spence. Also included are poems by Sterling A. Brown, Langston Hughes, and Jessie Fauset.
- Love and the difficulties of life during the Harlem Renaissance
- Performed without breaks or an intermission to unify what might otherwise feel disjointed

1935

Mulatto: A Tragedy of the Deep South - Langston Hughes

- Follows the story of a slave, Cora Lewis, who has four children with Colonel Norwood, the owner of the Plantation on which she lives
- Deals with issues such as employment, inheritance, social standing, justice, and suicide as a person of mixed race

1937

Golden Boy - Clifford Odets
- Focuses on Joe Wellington, a young Black man from Harlem who, despite his family's objections, turns to prizefighting as a means of escaping his ghetto roots and finding fame and fortune
- Redeveloped and staged as a musical in 1964 with a book by Clifford Odets and William Gibson, lyrics by Lee Adams, and music by Charles Strouse
  - Romance between Joe and Lorna, a white woman, developed into an explicit love affair culminating in a kiss that shocked audiences already having difficulty adjusting to a heavily urban jazz score and mentions of Malcolm X

1938

Big White Fog - Theodore Ward
- Ward's first major work
- Follows the fictional Mason family across three generations between 1922 and 1933. Half of the family supports a return to Africa and Garveyism, while the other half of the family seeks the American Dream.

1941

Native Son - Paul Green & Richard Wright
- Based on Richard Wright's novel of the same name
- A tormented Black man living in the slums of South Side Chicago is wanted for killing a white woman
- Produced and directed by Orson Welles. Also produced by John Houseman
- A powerful commentary on the American racial environment

1945

Deep Are the Roots - Arnaud d'Usseau & James Gow
- Decorated African American Army sergeant returns home after WWII. Having been in command overseas Brett resists being "put in his place" in his segregated hometown. An interracial romance complicates things further.

1946

Jeb - Robert Ardrey

- Trouble ensues when a Black soldier returns home from the war with a disability but also a skill that is considered the domain of the white man, the expert use of an adding machine. Relentless opposition leaves him physically beaten but undefeated as he prepares to head to the South to help in the larger cause of racism.
- The story of the making of a militant

1951

The Same Sky - Yvonne Mitchell

- Set in London in 1940 during The Blitz. At the center is the romance between a young couple, Esther Brodsky, who is Jewish, and Jeff Smith, who is not. Initially the families are opposed to the relationship, but only after Jeff is killed in the war do they become reconciled

1954

The Amen Corner - James Baldwin

- Follows the story of church pastor Margaret Alexander on her journey to the realization that she should not use religion as an excuse to escape the struggles of life and love
- Addresses themes of the role of the church in the African American family, and the effect of poverty born of racial prejudice on the African American community
- Baldwin's first attempt at theatre after his first success as a novelist

1958

A Taste of Honey - Shelagh Delaney

- A working-class, adolescent girl and her relationships with the Black sailor who makes her pregnant, the homosexual art student who moves into her apartment to help her through her pregnancy, her fun-loving, saloon-frequenting mother, and her mother's newly acquired husband.
- British dramatist. Written when she was 19-years-old

- Highlights the social tensions of class, race, gender, and sexual orientation in Britain during this time period.

The World of Suzie Wong - Paul Osborn

- A painter, looking for inspiration for his art, unknowingly rents a room in a Hong Kong bordello and falls for a kind-hearted prostitute.

- Audience success but an example of the stereotypical and demeaning ways Asian women are portrayed.

1959

The Death of Bessie Smith - Edward Albee

- Set in 1937 in Memphis, Tennessee, in a segregated hospital, the play tells the story of the death of singer Bessie Smith following a car crash after she was refused admittance to a white hospital.

- Premise was largely accepted as fact until convincing evidence to the contrary appeared in the original 1972 edition of *Bessie*, a biography of the singer.

- The character of Bessie Smith is only referred to in Albee's play and does not appear on stage.

A Majority of One - Leonard Spigelgass

- A Jewish widow is convinced by her daughter to move from Brooklyn to Tokyo in order to be closer. The daughter's husband is stationed at the U.S. Embassy there. The widow's feelings about the Japanese whom she holds responsible for her son's death in WWII start to change on board the ship where she meets a Japanese businessman who also lost a spouse and two children in the war. A bond and then a romance develop, and her daughter and son-in-law object to the idea of an interracial marriage.

A Raisin in the Sun - Lorraine Hansberry

- Examines the effects of racial prejudice on the fulfillment of an African American family's dreams

- Centers around the Youngers, a working-class family that lives in Chicago's South Side during the mid-twentieth century. Having just lost their patriarch, Big Walter, they are awaiting an insurance check, but each family member's differing ideas about what to do with the money causes tension.

1960

A Passage to India - Santha Rama Rau

- Two English women make the journey to 1920s India. While on a hike one of them is attacked in a cave and assumes it is by the Indian doctor that guides them. She testifies against him in court and the trial becomes a media sensation that reinforces tensions between the British Empire and the Indian independence movement.
- Based on an E.M. Forster novel

1961

Andorra - Max Frisch

- Written fifteen years after the end of World War II, the play serves as more of a study of cultural prejudice than a specific reflection on the war. However, it concerns more than just prejudice: many of the characters have something to gain from main character Andri's being a Jew.
- The motif of whitewashing, with which the play starts and ends, also points to hypocrisy as a central theme.

Call Me by My Rightful Name - Michael Shurtleff

- Set in the early 1960s, the play centers around two Columbia roommates, a white graduate student and an African American undergraduate caught in a love triangle over a white woman. When the two disagree on their definitions of love, a fight ensues, forcing Chris – the object of their affection – to act as peacemaker. The shame and misconceptions of both young men are explored with devastating honesty.

Mandingo - Jack Kirkland

- An African slave is trained to fight other slaves on an antebellum Southern plantation
- Adapted into a film by Paramount Pictures in 1975

Purlie Victorious - Ossie Davis

- Set during the Jim Crow era, the play follows traveling preacher Purlie Victorious Judson, who returns to his small Georgia town hoping to save Big Bethel, the community's church, and emancipate the cotton pickers who work on oppressive Ol' Cap'n Cotchipee's plantation

- Developed into a musical in 1970 with a book by Ossie Davis, Philip Rose, and Peter Udell, lyrics by Udell and music by Gary Geld

1964

Blues for Mister Charlie - James Baldwin
- A "social commentary drama in three acts"
- Dedicated to the memory of Medgar Evers, his widow and children, and to the memory of the dead children of Birmingham
- Loosely based on the Emmett Till murder that occurred in Money, Mississippi, before the Civil Rights Movement began
- Baldwin and Evers were close friends

Dutchman - Amiri Baraka
- A one-act allegory depicting Black and white relations during the time it was written
- Set in a New York City subway car, the play involves Clay, a young, middle-class Black man who is approached seductively by Lula, a white fellow passenger. They flirt, she provokes Clay to anger, and finally murders him

Funnyhouse of a Negro - Adrienne Kennedy
- Tells the story of a young Black woman named Sarah living in New York City, and focuses on her internal struggle with racial identity
- Takes place in Sarah's mind, allowing the audience to witness the anxiety, entrapment, and alienation of being a Black woman in the United States. Kennedy focuses on the obsession with whiteness and the struggle of mixed ancestry
- Written during the Black Arts Movement of the 1960s and early 1970s, which had a strong masculine element, Kennedy's female perspective was a rarity for the time and the movement

1966

A Hand Is on the Gate - Roscoe Lee Browne
- An eight-person cast reads writings by African American authors and performs traditional African American songs

The Indian Wants the Bronx - Israel Horovitz
- Centers around two teenagers who confront and eventually attack an Indian man trying to visit his son in New York City

- Main theme of communication, as their inability to communicate results in a tragic conclusion

---

1967

The Great White Hope - Howard Sackler
- Based on the true story of prizefighter Jack Johnson and his first wife, Etta Terry Duryea, the controversy over their marriage and Duryea's death by suicide in 1912
- The term "the great white hope" is a reference to the white boxer who many hoped would finally defeat Johnson, which reflects the racism and segregation of the era in which Jack Johnson fought
- Adapted into a film in 1970

Los Vendidos - Luis Valdez
- Examines stereotypes of Latinos in California and how they are treated by local, state, and federal governments

One Last Look - Steve Carter
- During a funeral service, members of two Black families reflect on the death of their common patriarch

---

1968

Carry Me Back to Morningside Heights - Robert Alan Aurthur
- A young Jewish man insists on becoming a slave to an African American law student as a personal penance for the years of atrocities white people have forced on Black people

Indians - Arthur Kopit
- Cast in the style of a vaudeville Wild West Show, this play explores the theme of America's mistreatment of the indigenious tribes

---

1969

Ceremonies in Dark Old Men - Lonne Elder III
- The play is a dramatization of rituals—of survival, of friendship, of deception and manipulation, of self-deception, of Black male friendship, of shifting intrafamilial allegiances, and of Black manhood
- Adapted into a television movie in 1975

1970

Les Blancs - Lorraine Hansberry
- Follows the experiences of settlers, natives, and an American journalist in an unnamed African country in the waning days of colonial control
- Hansberry's only play that takes place in Africa and uses both dance and music as signifiers of Black and African cultures, a concept called the Black Aesthetic

1971

Black Girl - J. E. Franklin
- A drama about a young Black woman who defies the low expectations thrust upon her by her unsupportive family and pursues her dream of becoming a ballet dancer

1972

The River Niger - Joseph A. Walker
- A young African-American who returns to his home in Harlem from the Air Force and becomes involved with a group of young revolutionaries.
- Focuses on themes common to much of Walker's work: the struggles of Black men in a racist society; the camaraderie between Black men; the role of men in the Black family; and efforts among African Americans to achieve greater equality

1974

The Year of the Dragon - Frank Chin
- One of the first plays by an Asian American playwright to be produced on a mainstream New York stage
- Critique of the racism in American society through satire surrounding American tourists who eroticize, objectify, and commodify Chinatown and its residents

1976

Eden - Steve Carter
- A recent Caribbean immigrant discovers that his daughter has fallen in love with an uneducated African American man from the rural South

For Colored Girls Who Have Considered Suicide / When the Rainbow Is Enuf - Ntozake Shange

- Tells the stories of seven women who have suffered oppression in a racist and sexist society
- Series of poetic monologues to be accompanied by dance movements and music, a form Shange coined as the "choreopoem for colored girls"

1978

Nevis Mountain Dew - Steve Carter

- Set in the Queens borough of New York City in 1954, a Caribbean-American family gathers to celebrate the 50th birthday of Jared Philibert, who is confined to an iron lung due to paralysis. Ayton, Jared's best friend, arrives at the party with a bottle of rum called "Nevis Mountain Dew." When people drink it, the rum seems to act as a truth serum.

1979

Full Frontal - Michael Hastings

- A monologue by Gabriel Nkoke, a man born in Nigeria but raised almost all his life in England, delivered to an unseen representative of the National Front, which Gabriel is at first seen trying to join because he agrees with their racialist agenda

Spell No. 7 - Ntozake Shange

- The story is about a group of Black friends who are actors, musicians, and performers. In a series of dreamlike vignettes and poetic monologues, they commiserate about the difficulties they face as Black artists.

Zoot Suit - Luis Valdez

- Tells the story of Henry Reyna and the 38th Street Gang, who were tried for the Sleepy Lagoon murder in Los Angeles, during World War II
- Details the discrimination that Los Angeles's Chicano population faced in the 1940s,

1980

Black Children's Day - Adrienne Kennedy

- Depicts a chaotic hour before the Children's Day Play. Features ten children playing various roles and one adult.

- Follows no real linear structure. Uses surrealism as an element to explore the American experience from a non-white perspective

1981

Dame Lorraine - Steve Carter

- Third of Carter's Caribbean trilogy (Steve Carter was best known for his plays involving Caribbean immigrants living in the United States)
- Tells the story of a family who has lost all of their sons, except one who is returning from a long sentence in prison

A Soldier's Play - Charles Fuller

- Uses a murder mystery to explore the complicated feelings of anger and resentment that some African Americans have toward one another, and the ways in which many Black Americans have absorbed white racist attitudes

1982

Jitney - August Wilson

- Portrays the lives of five Black jitney drivers at a station in Pittsburgh's Hill District. They fight for love, survival, and respect as they face closure.
- Deals with the gradual gentrification of the Hill District and the economic and psychological oppression that weighs down and sometimes divides the Black community

One Monkey Don't Stop No Show - Don Evans

- Satirical comedy about middle-class Black Philadelphians thrown into moral chaos when the prospect of sex rears its head and a preacher's virgin niece from the rural South hooks up with his dead brother's business partner in a shady nightclub

1984

Joe Turner's Come and Gone - August Wilson

- Major themes of identity, migration, and racial discrimination
  - Each of the characters is seeking identity as an American, African, man, woman, businessman, and/or artist
  - Migration is seen in the shuffling of people after the emancipation of the slaves which caused many social and cultural issues throughout the nation

      o Even though there seems to be a promise of jobs and freedom in the North, it often seems as racially divided as the South

---

1985

Fences - August Wilson
- 6th play in Wilson's Pittsburgh cycle
- Explores the evolving African American experience and examines race relations, among other themes
- Tells the story of a Black trash collector who dreamed of being in Major League Baseball. Though unable to break that color barrier, he does become the first Black garbage truck driver. The choices he makes and tries to force on his family create emotional fences that drive them apart.

1986

Dreaming Emmett - Toni Morrison
- An historical retelling of the life of Emmett Till, a 14-year-old African-American boy beaten to death in 1955 by a group of white men, and the subsequent trial and acquittal of his killers

---

1987

Driving Miss Daisy - Alfred Uhry
- An elderly Jewish widow living in Atlanta, is determined to maintain her independence. However, when she crashes her car, her son arranges for her to have a chauffeur, an African-American driver. Their relationship gets off to a rocky start, but over the course of 25 years, they gradually form a close friendship, one that transcends racial prejudices and social conventions.
- The optimism of racial progress as told by a white writer and director. Reinforces the belief that prolonged exposure to the Black person will enhance the humanity of the white person in the friendship.
- Ignores the transactional nature of the employer/employee relationship

The Meeting - Jeff Stetson
- An imagined meeting of Dr. King and Malcolm X in a Harlem hotel on Valentine's Day 1965, a week before the assassination of Malcolm X

The Piano Lesson - August Wilson

- A play featuring a strong female character to confront African American history
- Follows the lives of the Charles family in the Doaker Charles household and an heirloom, the family piano, which is decorated with designs carved by an enslaved ancestor
- Focuses on the arguments between a brother and a sister who have different ideas on what to do with the piano

1990

Pecong - Steve Carter

- Set on a fictional Caribbean Island, it tells the story of a sorceress who falls madly in love with a shallow womanizer
- A faithful reboot of the Medea story from Greek myth set in a Black world
- Focuses on themes of sex and power

Pill Hill - Sam Kelley

- Examines the failures, successes, and relationships of six Black steel mill workers in Chicago as they transition from blue-collar jobs to white-collar professions
- The Pill Hill neighborhood in Chicago was a symbol of affluence that represented the American Dream. For young Black individuals, this symbol was especially poignant, which provides much of the subtext of the play.

Six Degrees of Separation - John Guare

- Explores the existential premise that everyone in the world is connected to everyone else in the world by a chain of no more than six acquaintances
- A young Black conman victimizes two households with no good outcome.

1992

Fires in the Mirror: Crown Heights, Brooklyn and Other Identities - Anna Deavere Smith

- Explores the 1991 Crown Heights riot and its aftermath through the viewpoints of African American and Jewish people, mostly based in New York City, who were connected directly and indirectly to the riot

1994

Twilight: Los Angeles, 1992 - Anna Deavere Smith

- About the 1992 Los Angeles riots

- Composed of a series of monologues by real people of all races connected directly and indirectly to the riots

1995

Seven Guitars - August Wilson
- Focuses on seven African American characters in the year 1948
- Recurring theme of the African American male's fight for his own humanity, self-understanding, and self-acceptance in the face of personal and societal ills

1996

Sisterella (musical) - Music, lyrics and book by Larry Hart
- A Gospel/R&B spoof of Cinderella from an African American perspective

Venus - Suzan-Lori Parks
- Response to some of the known historical events that occurred to a Khoisan woman known as Saartjie Baartman/The Venus Hottentot
- Uses the concept of Baartman's career to explore colonization, racial objectification, and historical sexualization of Black female bodies

Without Skin or Breathlessness - Tanya Barfield
- A young girl is trying to cope with her social alienation as a child of mixed heritage; her white mother is struggling with a terminal disease; and her black father is confronting unemployment

1998

I Know I've Been Changed - Tyler Perry
- Tells the story of two adult survivors of child abuse who became the people that their abusive mother said they would be

1999

James Baldwin: A Soul on Fire - Howard Simon
- Uses spirituals to evoke the Black liberation struggle and to create audience involvement

Offensive Fouls - Jason Long

- Follows Joey as he is benched from his basketball team after Christine suspects that he was involved in a racially motivated corner-store vandalism incident

Spinning into Butter - Rebecca Gilman

- A searing, comic expose of political correctness at a small New England college. A crisis erupts when racist notes are posted on the dorm room door of one of the school's few African American students.
- Treatment of racism in the play has sparked some controversy (arguments over whether it exposes or perpetuates racism)
- The title refers to an old folktale considered racist, *Little Black Sambo.*

I Can Do Bad All by Myself - Tyler Perry

- First official appearance of the well-known fictional character Madea. Madea's family comes to see her while she's sick, however it's the rest of the family that needs help.
- Perry is an entertainment juggernaut who employs the Black community but is criticized for stereotypical and buffoonish portrayals of African Americans

King Hedley II - August Wilson

- Tells the story of an ex-con in Pittsburgh trying to rebuild his life
- Examines African American life in the United States during the twentieth century

2001

Da Kink in My Hair - Trey Anthony

- Novelette is forced to confront her goals and ideals in life when she receives news that her onetime boyfriend Cedric, who loaned her the money to open a hair salon, has died and his daughter Verena is demanding repayment of the loan

Diary of a Mad Black Woman - Tyler Perry

- Helen McCarter has everything a woman wants: a nice house and a rich husband. After admitting to an affair, her husband throws her out of the house. She turns to her mother, grandmother Madea, and cousin Brian who take her in and turn her back to God

2002

Yellowman - Dael Orlandersmith

- Details the relationship between Eugene, a very fair-skinned Black man, and Alma, a large, dark-skinned woman

2003

Gem of the Ocean - August Wilson

- The 9th play written in his decade-by-decade, ten-play chronicle, The Pittsburgh Cycle, dramatizing the African American experience in the twentieth century. However, it chronicles the first decade, the 1900s.
- set in 1904 in Pittsburgh's Hill District, Aunt Ester, the drama's 285-year-old fiery matriarch, welcomes into her home Solly Two Kings, who was born into slavery and scouted for the Union Army, and Citizen Barlow, a young man searching for redemption and a new life.

Intimate Apparel - Lynn Nottage

- Set in New York City in 1905 and concerns a young African American woman who is disappointed in love but pursues her dreams of independence as an in-demand seamstress.
- Based on Nottage's great-grandmother

Platanos Y Collard Greens - David Lamb

- Explores relations between African Americans and Latinos in New York City through a relationship between two college students

Talk - Carl Hancock Rux

- Controversial African American writer is found dead in his prison cell. A young artist has gathered five panelists to discuss the life and work of the writer and the meaning of his legacy.
- A fierce exploration of identity, and the struggle to maintain an original voice.

2004

Meet the Browns - Tyler Perry

- A continuation of the Madea family chronicles, this one brings everyone together after a death in the family. Coming together for the funeral will be harder than it sounds. Through all the drama and commotion they find love and know that there's nothing like family and prayer.

*N*gger Wetb*ck Ch*nk: The Race Play* - Rafael Agustin, Allan Axibal, Miles Gregley, Liesel Reinhart, & Steven T. Seagle

- Traces the origins and evolution of three derogatory terms that have shaped the lives of minorities in the hope of stripping these words of their power

2005

The Dance: The History of American Minstrelsy - Jason Christophe White
- An educational play based upon the history of American Minstrelsy, conveyed to the audience from the perspectives of two stock minstrel clowns, who perform this history as a historic minstrel production

Deep Azure - Chadwick Boseman
- The story of an anorexic-bulimic African American woman whose fiancé is killed by a black police officer
- Highlights struggles of body image and beauty, issues that are often ignored by the misogynistic brand of Hip Hop, and also illuminates the topical issues of racial profiling and police brutality

Hazzard County - Allison Moore
- Centers on a young widowed mother and a visit she receives from a big city television producer
- Takes a deep look at southern "Good Ole Boy" culture and its popularization through the lens of American mass media

Nowhere on the Border - Carlos Lacamara
- One-act play written by American playwright Carlos Lacamara in response to the Immigration conflict

Radio Golf - August Wilson
- Final installment in his ten-part series, *The Century Cycle*
- Harmond Wilks, an Ivy League-educated Black man who has inherited a real estate agency from his father, his ambitious wife Mame, and his friend Roosevelt Hicks want to redevelop the Hill District in Pittsburgh, Pennsylvania

This Is How It Goes - Neil LaBute
- About the repercussions of an interracial love triangle in small town America

2006

Thurgood - George Stevens, Jr.
- One-man play about the life of Thurgood Marshall, the first African American to serve on the U.S. Supreme Court
- A filmed version of the play aired by HBO was described by the Baltimore Sun as "one of the most frank, informed and searing discussions of race you will ever see on TV."

What's Done in the Dark - Tyler Perry

- A mixture of comedy, drama, and music, set in a hospital emergency room. Focuses on two nurses, one is a single mother and the other is having an affair with a doctor, and on an eccentric, hypochondriac patient who is in fact, Mr. Brown from the Madea family of characters

---

2007

Dance Without Movement - Sophia Rashid

- A one-woman play. Zuleikha's Pakistani background and Muslim faith are at odds with her English upbringing. Amidst a sea of confusion Zuleikha must try to unravel her true identity.

A Disappearing Number - directed and conceived by Simon McBurney, co-written and devised by the Théâtre de Complicité company

- Inspired by the collaboration during the 1910s between the pure mathematicians Srinivasa Ramanujan from India, and the Cambridge University don G.H. Hardy
- Mathematical theory becomes a metaphor for the Indian diaspora

Hoodoo Love - Katori Hall

- Tells the story of an aspiring African American singer in Memphis, who seeks help with her personal life from a local hoodoo practitioner

Statement of Regret - Kwame Kwei-Armah

- Kwaku Mackenzie, founder of a Black policy think tank, hits the bottle after his father's death, causing his institute to flounder. In a vain attempt to regain influence, he publicly champions division within the Black community, and the consequences are shattering.

Why Did I Get Married? - Tyler Perry

- When a young temptress threatens an already troubled marriage, a close-knit family rallies together to examine their own marriages and to rediscover the precious reason that the one they have is the one they want forever

Yellow Face - David Henry Hwang

- Semi-autobiographical play by David Henry Hwang, featuring the author himself as the protagonist, DHH, mounting his 1993 play Face Value
- Themes include questions of race and of the interaction between media and politics

2008

Lucky You - Denis Calandra & Francis Matthews

- Several residents of Grange, famous for its miracles, share a winning lottery number. Mayhem ensues as they fight over the $28 million jackpot
- Based on a Carl Hiaasen novel with its share of colorful buffoons, rednecks, white-supremacists, etc. there are serious themes beneath the comedy

Marilyn and Ella - Bonnie Greer

- Musical drama about the friendship between Marilyn Monroe and Ella Fitzgerald

The Monkey Jar - Richard Martin Hirsch

- A public elementary school is thrown into upheaval when a ten-year old Asian American student is accused of pulling a gun on his possibly abusive, gay, fourth-grade teacher

Ruined - Lynn Nottage

- Set in the Democratic Republic of Congo, the play revolves around the women of a brothel/bar that services both the government soldiers and the rebels, leading to close calls that add tension to an already fraught situation. In the course of the play we learn the heart-wrenching stories of these women who are caught in the crossfire of the men's war. They have been forced into a life of prostitution because they see it as their only chance for survival.
- Nottage hoped that her play would call attention to the plight of the Congo and its raging war that had been largely ignored by the international community

Superior Donuts - Tracy Letts

- Focuses on the relationship between despondent Arthur Przybyszewski, a former 1960s radical who owns a rundown donut shop in Uptown Chicago, and Franco, his energetic but troubled young African American assistant, who wants to update the establishment with lively music and healthy menu options
- Although the play does delve into issues of race and politics, many critics consider *Donuts* closer to a TV sitcom rather than a brilliant piece of theater.

2009

Anne and Emmett - Janet Langhart Cohen

- An imaginary conversation between Anne Frank and Emmett Till, both victims of racial intolerance and hatred

Fly - Trey Ellis & Ricardo Khan

- Play about the Tuskegee Airmen, the first black fliers in the U.S. military during World War II
- while the fight against racism is central to the play's story, the pursuit of any dream is also a key theme

Laugh to Keep from Crying - Tyler Perry

- A mixture of comedy, drama, and music, set at an inner-city building in a predominantly African American neighborhood

Monday - Gloria Idahota Williams

- A one-woman stage play in which a disturbing series of events harms and eventually destroys the world of what appears to everyone else to be a typical, church-going North London, Jamaican family

The Mountaintop - Katori Hall

- A fictional depiction of Martin Luther King Jr.'s last night on earth set entirely in Room 306 of the Lorraine Motel on the eve of his assassination in 1968

Race - David Mamet

- A racially charged sex crime takes place which leads to charges being made against Charles Strickland, a wealthy resident in his town
- In Mamet's own words, the "theme [of the play] is race and the lies we tell each other on the subject"

2010

...And Jesus Moonwalks the Mississippi - Marcus Gardley

- A re-imagining of the Greek myth of Persephone and Demeter, in which a lynched African American man named Damascus is immediately resurrected as a woman named Demeter, who only has three days to find her daughter Po'em and transmit her song before she has to return to death

Clybourne Park - Bruce Norris

- Portrays fictional events set during and after *A Raisin in the Sun* in the same house portrayed in that play. Loosely based on historical events that took place in the city of Chicago
- According to *The Washington Post*, the play "applies a modern twist to the issues of race and housing and aspirations for a better life"

A Free Man of Color - John Guare
- Story follows main character Jacques Cornet, the wealthiest Black man in New Orleans at the time of the Louisiana Purchase, and his experiences with racism

The Scottsboro Boys (musical) - book by David Thompson, music by John Kander and lyrics by Fred Ebb
- Based on the Scottsboro Boys trial, the musical has the framework of a minstrel show, altered to "create a musical social critique" with a company that, except for one, consists entirely of Black performers
- The trial it is based on was a miscarriage of justice, a national outrage, and helped jumpstart the American civil rights movement.

Sucker Punch - Roy Williams
- Set in a run-down London boxing ring in the 1980s, two young black boys, Leon and Troy, are trained by a white trainer, Charlie, who sees potential in both of them. The boys' paths diverge, but eventually they are pitted against each other to fight.

2011

Mogadishu - Vivienne Franzmann
- A white teacher tries to protect her black student from expulsion after he pushes her to the ground, to which the student responds by dragging her into a vortex of lies in which victim becomes perpetrator

The Haves and the Have Nots - Tyler Perry
- Follows the life of a wealthy family confronted with the needs of their poverty-stricken housekeeper
- *Stick Fly* - Lydia Diamond
- The affluent, African American LeVay family, the first Black family on Martha's Vineyard, is gathering for the weekend. The two brothers have brought their girlfriends home to meet the parents for the first time
- The girlfriends butt heads over issues of race, privilege, and gender politics as long standing family tensions bubble under the surface and reach a boiling point

2012

Disgraced - Ayad Akhtar
- Surrounds a dinner party between four different people with very different backgrounds

- Centered on sociopolitical themes such as Islamophobia and the self-identity of Muslim-American citizens
- Depicts racial and ethnic prejudices that "secretly persist in even the most progressive cultural circles"

The Fortress of Solitude (musical) - music and lyrics written by Michael Friedman, book by Itamar Moses

- Follows Dylan Ebdus, a white kid growing up in a mostly black section of Gowanus, Brooklyn in the late 1970s
- Exposes the cruel gravitational pull of class and race in America

---

2013

One Night in Miami - Kemp Powers

- Imagines a meeting between four, still nascent, Black American icons Malcolm X, Muhammad Ali, James Brown, and Sam Cooke at a pivotal moment in their views on civil rights and their roles going forward.

The Secret River - Andrew Bovell

- A man is exiled from London in the eighteenth century and is sent with his family to a penal colony in the Hawkesbury River, New South Wales, where he hopes to make a new start, but its inhabitants, the indigenous Dharug people, are not willing to give up their

Land

- Explores the injustice and brutality of colonialism

2014

Blood at the Root - Dominique Morisseau

- Based on the Jena Six case, which created a great deal of tension in Louisiana in 2006.
- Scrutinizes the intrinsic links between justice, bias, and identity

Hell Hath No Fury Like a Woman Scorned - Tyler Perry

- Anita, a single, Black woman, meets a man online thanks to encouragement from a friend. At first he treats her like a queen. Then they get married, and things change. Anita takes her life back in unpredictable and entertaining ways.

2015

Sweat - Lynn Nottage
- Centered on the working class of Reading, Pennsylvania
- Examines the disintegration of friendship as management/worker pressures and job migration to foreign countries begins to drive a wedge. Racial tensions separate them further.

2017

The Lynching: What They Wouldn't Let Jackie Walker Tell You - Jackie Walker
- A one-person play by British activist Jackie Walker
- Focuses on the lives of Walker's activist parents, her own struggles with racism after she came to Britain in the late 1950s, and what happened to her after the Labour Party was accused of antisemitism

Pipeline - Dominique Morisseau
- A mother's hopes for her son clash with an educational system rigged against him

2018

Calpurnia - Audrey Dwyer
- Julie, a twenty-something Black woman living in Toronto with her father, an Afro-Caribbean judge, is a screenwriter attempting to write a film about Calpurnia, the Finches' maid in *To Kill A Mockingbird*

Fairview - Jackie Sibblies Drury
- A middle class African American family prepares for a birthday dinner for their grandmother only to be watched by four white people
- Plays with the reality that typical theatre-goers are white and affluent by making it the point of the play. The actors start the play performing for the audience and then break the fourth wall and ask the audience to perform for the performers and for each other.

Slave Play - Jeremy O. Harris
- Follows three interracial couples undergoing "Antebellum Sexual Performance Therapy" because the Black partners no longer feel sexual attraction to their white partners

- The title refers both to the history of slavery in the United States and to sexual slavery role-play
- Deals with themes of race, sex, power relations, trauma, and interracial relationships

Soft Power (musical) - book and lyrics by David Henry Hwang and music and additional lyrics by Jeanine Tesori

- Instead of exoticizing an Asian country, Soft Power exoticizes America by looking at it from a hypothetical future Chinese musical

---

2019

The Haunting of Lin-Manuel Miranda - Ishmael Reed

- Critiques *Hamilton* through a depiction of a fictionalized version of *Hamilton*'s creator Lin-Manuel Miranda, who is visited by several historical figures missing from the musical in a style similar to Charles Dickens' *A Christmas Carol*

A COUPLE OF GREATS

Paul Robeson

Concert artist, actor, and activist Paul Leroy Robeson was born on April 9, 1898 in Princeton, New Jersey to William Robeson, a church minister and former slave,[33] and Maria Bustill, a member of the prominent Bustill Quaker family.[34, 35] Even during high school, Robeson showed an affinity to the arts, performing in school plays and singing in chorus, while also excelling in sports.[36] He graduated as valedictorian, and earned a scholarship to Rutgers College,[37] where he was the third ever African-American student to

[33] Nollen, Scott Allen (October 14, 2010). Paul Robeson: Film Pioneer. McFarland. ISBN 978-0786457472.

[34] Robeson, Paul Jr. (July 9, 2001). The Undiscovered Paul Robeson, An Artist's Journey, 1898–1939. John Wiley & Sons. ISBN 978-0471151050.

[35] Brown, Lloyd Louis (1997). The Young Paul Robeson: "on My Journey Now". Westview Press. ISBN 978-0813331775.

[36] Boyle, Sheila Tully; Bunie, Andrew (October 1, 2005). Paul Robeson: The Years of Promise and Achievement. University of Massachusetts Press. ISBN 978-1558495050.

[37] Brown, Lloyd Louis (1997). The Young Paul Robeson: "on My Journey Now". Westview Press. ISBN 978-0813331775.

ever enroll.[38] He excelled at Rutgers in both academics and extracurriculars,[39] and again graduated as valedictorian (Robe). Robeson went on to pursue law at Columbia Law School (Brown), during which time he was also selected to play in the NFL whilst completing his studies,[40] and performed in theater productions in both the U.S. and U.K. (Dub). In 1921, he married Eslanda Goode, with whom he eventually had one son, Paul Robeson Jr., in 1927 (Robeson).

While he forewent a career in law for various reasons, including racism in the field,[41] Robeson received plenty of theater career opportunities, making appearances in productions such as *All God's Chillun Got Wings* and *The Emperor Jones,* and films such as *Body and Soul* (Nollen). He experienced great success in such roles, and was quickly welcomed into the circle of social elites,[42] a trajectory that was heavily directed by his wife who eventually became his agent (Robe). One of his most notable roles was playing Joe in *Show Boat*, playing more than 350 performances at the Theatre Royal in London and earning him a summons for a Royal Command Performance at Buckingham Palace, as well as acquaintanceship with House of Commons parliament members (Dub, Boyle). Eslanda was aware of Robeson having extramarital affairs, but did not act on it until she found out he had one with his fellow cast member, Peggy Ashcroft, after which he and his wife finally divorced (Robeson).

Robeson became more politically active and attached to his heritage roots over the years, joining the anti-imperialism movement, enrolling in the School or Oriental and African Studies, and aligning himself with political causes, much to the dismay of his business agent (Nollen). He appreciated the socialist values of the Soviet Union,[43] siding with the Republican cause and refugees of the Spanish Civil War, supporting Jawaharlal Nehru and Indian independence, and advocating for labor unions (Robe, Dub). Robeson continued to act and tour, while promoting social justice causes at every turn, especially in advocating for rights and respect for Black people. During World War II, he did charity

---

[38] Duberman, Martin B. (1989). Paul Robeson. Bodley Head. ISBN 978-0370305752.

[39] "Men of the Month". The Crisis. Vol. 15 no. 5. March 1918. pp. 229–31. ISSN 0011-1422.; cf. Marable 2005, p. 171

[40] Levy, Alan H. (2003). Tackling Jim Crow, Racial Segregation in Professional Football. McFarland and Co., Inc. ISBN 0-7864-1597-5.

[41] Gilliam, Dorothy Butler (1978). Paul Robeson: All-American. New Republic Book Company.

[42] Sampson, Henry T. (2005). Swingin' on the Ether Waves: A Chronological History of African Americans in Radio and Television Programming, 1925–1955. Scarecrow Press. ISBN 978-0810840874.

[43] Robeson, Paul (1978a). Sheldon, Philip; Foner, Henry (eds.). Paul Robeson Speaks: Writings, Speeches, and Interviews, a Centennial Celebration. Citadel Press. ISBN 978-0806508153.

performances to support the war effort, but was still targeted by the U.S. government due to his radical beliefs and affiliations with Communism. His passport was denied and he was blacklisted, as the government attempted to defame him.[44] The Soviet Union awarded him the International Stalin Prize. He sidestepped the travel ban by performing transatlantic telephone concerts.[45] He finally performed world tours again after his passport was reinstated in 1958, though his health deteriorated during these travels and he was frequently hospitalized (R, D). He returned to America for retirement, after which he made few appearances, except for civil rights causes (D). He died on January 23, 1976 after a stroke.

---

[44] Wright, Charles H. (January 1, 1975). Robeson: Labor's Forgotten Champion. Balamp Publishing Company. ISBN 978-0913642061.

[45] Presenters: Aleks Krotoski (January 5, 2016). "Hidden Histories of the Information Age: TAT-1". Hidden Histories of the Information Age. 9:50 minutes in. BBC Radio 4. Archived from the original on June 20, 2015.

Marian Anderson

Marian Anderson (1897-1993) was born in Philadelphia. When she was 6, she became a choir member at the Union Baptist Church. Her father supported her music interests and, when she was 8, bought her a piano. Although her father died a few years later, Anderson remained deeply committed to music. Her commitment and range as a singer impressed her choir so much that the church raised enough money for her to train under Giuseppe Boghetti, a respected voice teacher.

After studying with Boghetti, Anderson won a chance to sing at the Lewisohn Stadium in New York. Other opportunities soon followed: in 1928, she performed at Carnegie Hall for the first time, and she eventually embarked on a tour through Europe thanks to a scholarship. In 1939, Anderson's manager tried to set up a performance for her at Washington, D.C.'s Constitution Hall. However, the Daughters of the American Revolution turned her away based on a policy that limited the hall to white performers only. When the public learned what had happened, an uproar ensued, in part by Eleanor Roosevelt, who invited Anderson to perform instead at the Lincoln Memorial on Easter Sunday. In front of a crowd of more than 75,000, Anderson delivered a riveting performance that was broadcast live for millions of radio listeners.

Throughout the next decades, Anderson's fame only grew. In 1961, she performed the national anthem at President John F. Kennedy's inauguration. Two years later, Kennedy honored her with the Presidential Medal of Freedom. Anderson retired in 1965 to a farm in Connecticut. In 1991, the music world honored her with a Grammy Award for Lifetime Achievement. Anderson spent her final years in Portland, Oregon, where she moved with her nephew. She died of natural causes on April 8, 1993.

FILM

American Films

1898

Black Cavalry Marching
- One of the first depictions of Black people on film
- Viewable at: https://www.loc.gov/item/00694179

Something Good Negro Kiss
- The first depiction of on-screen Black love and possibly the first-known Black film
- Known for departing from the prevalent and purely stereotypical presentation of racist caricature in popular culture at the time it was made
- Viewable at: https://vimeo.com/305144396

1912

The Railroad Porter
- First film with an all-Black cast and production company

1914

Uncle Tom's Cabin
- Based upon playwright George L. Aiken's theatrical adaptation of Harriet Beecher Stowe's 1852 novel *Uncle Tom's Cabin*
- First movie in which a Black actor was cast in a leading role in mainstream film (Sam Lucas)

1915

The Birth of a Nation
- First 12-reel film ever made and, at three hours, also the longest up to that point
- Pioneered close-ups, fade-outs, and a carefully staged battle sequence with hundreds of extras
- Has been called "the most controversial film ever made in the United States"
  - Black leaders tried to have it banned on the basis that it inflamed racial tensions and could incite violence

- o The White House held a private screening where President Woodrow Wilson said that the portrayal of Black people as predators was accurate
- Viewable at: https://archive.org/details/dw_griffith_birth_of_a_nation

---

1916

Intolerance
- Met with an enthusiastic reception from film critics upon its premiere and went on to be regarded as one of the most influential films of the silent era
- Explores the theme of intolerance partly in response to D.W. Griffith's previous film *The Birth of a Nation* being criticized by the NAACP and other groups for perpetuating racial stereotypes and glorifying the Ku Klux Klan
  - o Made it clear that the film was a rebuttal to his critics, as he felt that they were, in fact, the intolerant ones
- Viewable at: https://archive.org/details/INTOLERANCE_201407

1919

Broken Blossoms
- Tells the story of young girl, Lucy Burrows, who is abused by her alcoholic prizefighting father, Battling Burrows, and meets Cheng Huan, a kind-hearted Chinese man who falls in love with her
- Released during a period of strong anti-Chinese feeling in the US, themes in the film include cruelty and injustice against the innocent
- Viewable at: https://archive.org/details/brokenblossoms1919

1920

Within Our Gates
- Oscar Micheaux's response to Birth of a Nation
- Portrays the contemporary racial situation in the United States during the early twentieth century, the years of Jim Crow, the revival of the Ku Klux Klan, the Great Migration of Blacks to cities of the North and Midwest, and the emergence of the "New Negro"
- The film portrays racial violence under white supremacy and the lynching of Black individuals

- Considered an important expression of African American life in the years immediately following World War I, when violent racist incidents occurred throughout the United States, but most frequently in the South
- Viewable at: https://archive.org/details/silent-within-our-gates

1925

Body and Soul

- Starred Paul Robesom in his film debut
- Silent "race film" (meaning it was initially intended for an African American audience) originally released only in cinemas catering to that audience
  - Initially denied approval by the Motion Picture Commission of the State of New York on the grounds it would "tend to incite to crime" and was "immoral" and "sacrilegious," so Micheaux was forced to re-edit the film twice before it was approved
- Viewable at: https://www.tcm.com/tcmdb/title/341114/body-and-soul#overview

1929

Hearts in Dixie

- First all-Black talking major studio production
- Celebrates African American music and dance
- The characters are portrayed as racial stereotypes in terms of the contemporary white images of the period

1933

The Emperor Jones

- First mainstream box office film to feature an African American in a starring role (Paul Robeson as Brutus), which was said to be "a feat not repeated for more than two decades in the U.S."
- Viewable at: https://www.criterion.com/films/807-the-emperor-jones

1936

Show Boat

- See 'Theatre' → 'Musical Theatre' → *Show Boat* for plot summary and significance

1939

Gone With the Wind

- Regarded as one of the greatest and highest grossing films of all time
- Simultaneously criticized as historical negationism glorifying slavery and credited with triggering changes in the way in which African Americans are depicted cinematically
- Viewable at: HBO Max, Amazon Prime, and Apple TV

1943

Hitler's Children

- Black-and-white propaganda film made by RKO Radio Pictures
- Known for its portrayal of brutalities associated with the Hitler Youth, represented particularly by two young participants

1947

Crossfire

- Film noir drama film which deals with the theme of antisemitism
- Originally a story about anti-homosexuality, later changed to antisemitism

Gentleman's Agreement

- Follows a journalist who poses as a Jew to research an exposé on the widespread distrust and dislike of Jews in New York City and other affluent communities
- Viewable at: Amazon Prime, Apple TV. YouTube

1949

Home of the Brave

- During WWII, racial tensions arise between the white soldiers of a reconnaissance platoon and the single Black member of the group.
- Based on a play by Arthur Laurents which featured the protagonist being Jewish, rather than Black
- Utilizes the recurrent theme of a diverse group of men being subjected to the horror of war and their individual reactions, in this case, to the hell of jungle combat against the Japanese in World War II
- Viewable at: Amazon Prime Video

Lost Boundaries

- Based on William Lindsay White's story of the same title, a nonfiction account of Dr. Albert C. Johnston and his family, who passed for white while living in New England in the 1930s and 1940s. Except for supporting roles, white actors were used in the film (whitewashing in film). This whitewashing of all the leading roles was greatly controversial.
- Viewable at: YouTube, Apple TV, Amazon Prime Video

Pinky

- Stars Jeanne Crain as the title character, a young light-skinned Black woman who passes for white
- Generated considerable controversy due to its subject of race relations and its casting of Crain to play a Black woman
- Viewable at: https://www.youtube.com/watch?v=P6X-uCP_1c0&ab_channel=AviKohn

1950

The Jackie Robinson Story

- Focuses on Jackie Robinson's struggle with bigotry as he becomes the first African American Major League Baseball player of the modern era
- Viewable at: https://www.youtube.com/watch?v=8jFjDnSRdgE&ab_channel= TheFilmDetective

No Way Out

- Tells the story of a doctor whose ethics are tested when confronted with racism while tending to slum residents
- Controversial in its "graphic representation of racial violence" in what director Joseph L. Mankiewicz termed "the absolute blood and guts of Negro hating"
- Viewable at: https://www.youtube.com/watch?v=AlpK2tOHLGA&ab_channel=Film NoirPublicDomain

1954

Salt of the Earth

- Mexican American mine workers protest unsafe conditions and unequal wages. When an injunction stops them from their protest, the women take over the picket line.
- One of the first films to show protagonists overcoming racial divisions to achieve success

- One of the first pictures to advance the feminist social and political point of view
- Viewable at: https://archive.org/details/clacinonl_SaltOfTheEarth

1956

Giant
- Focuses on the struggle between wealthy oilmen and cattlemen in Texas in the mid to late 20th century
- Prejudice against Mexicans and an interracial marriage are sources of key conflict
- Viewable at: HBO Max

1958

The Defiant Ones
- Tells the story of two escaped prisoners, one white and one Black, who are shackled together and who must cooperate in order to survive
- Critical and Box Office success with many Academy Award nominations including Sidney Poitier for Best Actor
- Viewable at: Peacock, YouTube, Amazon Prime Video

1959

The Crimson Kimono
- Film noir thriller about a Caucasian and a Japanese American detective, partnered to solve a case, who both fall in love with a key witness
- Featured several ahead-of-its-time ideas about race and society's perception of race, a thematic and stylistic trademark of director Samuel Fuller
- Viewable at: YouTube, Apple TV, Amazon Prime Video

Imitation of Life
- An aspiring white actress takes in an African American widow whose mixed-race daughter is desperate to be seen as white
- Dealt with issues of race, class, and gender
- Viewable at: YouTube, Apple TV, Amazon Prime Video

Shadows
- Concerns race relations during the Beat Generation years in New York City

- Shocking to American audiences in the late 1950s and early 1960s because it featured an interracial couple in which the man does not realize that his love interest is of mixed race
- Viewable at: https://www.dailymotion.com/video/x2eoadq

1960

Sergeant Rutledge

- A respected Black cavalry sergeant stands court-martial for raping and killing a white woman and her father, his superior officer.
- One of the first mainstream films in the U.S. to treat racism frankly and to give a starring role to an African American actor
- Viewable at: Apple TV, Amazon Prime Video

1961

Bridge to the Sun

- Details the events of the life of a white American woman who marries a Japanese diplomat before World War II. Their cultures clash even as their countries become embroiled in war with each other
- Viewable at: YouTube, Apple TV, Amazon Prime Video

Paris Blues

- Deals with American racism of the time contrasted with Paris's open acceptance of Black people
- Viewable at: https://www.youtube.com/watch?v=gWQ5Oa33U9s&ab_channel=pumovie

A Raisin in the Sun

- Based on Lorraine Hansberry's 1959 play of the same name, it follows a Black family that wants a better life away from the South side of Chicago. A check that provides the financial means to achieve their dreams uncovers great tensions in the family.
- Explores the desire for social progress and the differing ideas about how to achieve it
- Viewable at: Vudu, Amazon Prime Video

West Side Story

- See 'Theatre' → 'Musical Theatre' → '*West Side Story*' for plot summary and significance
- Viewable at: Amazon Prime Video

1962

The Intruder

- Depicts the machinations of a racist named Adam Cramer, who arrives in the fictitious small Southern town of Caxton in order to incite white townspeople to racial violence against black townspeople and court-ordered school integration
- Viewable at: Amazon Prime Video

Pressure Point

- Drama about a Black prison psychiatrist assigned to treat an American Nazi sympathizer during World War II
- Sidney Poitier cast though the part was not written for a Black actor
- Viewable at: https://www.youtube.com/watch?v=A2_PMwOtA98&ab_channel=GilaEric

To Kill a Mockingbird

- Based on the novel by Harper Lee, a young girl nicknamed Scout recounts her coming of age in the Jim Crow South as her widowed father defends a Black man charged with raping a white woman.
- Portrays racism as seen through the innocent eyes of a child
- Viewable at: https://www.pbs.org/video/to-kill-a-mockingbird-1962-lnfoaz/

1963

Lilies of the Field

- A Black itinerant worker, played by Sidney Poitier, encounters a group of East German nuns, who believe he has been sent to them by God to build them a new chapel
- The racial significance of this film is that race is never mentioned in it as an issue
- Poitier won an Academy Award for his performance, the first African American actor to do so.
- Viewable at: Apple TV, Vudu, Amazon Prime Video

Shock Corridor

- Psychological thriller that tells the story of a journalist who gets himself intentionally committed to a mental hospital in order to solve a murder committed within the institution. Inside, he encounters patients who embody the psychopathy of xenophobia and racism in modern society in unique ways.

- Viewable at: https://www.youtube.com/watch?v=hBFBl_oP68c&ab_channel=cineufsc

1964

Black Like Me
- A journalist disguises himself to pass as an African American man for six weeks in 1959 in the Deep South in order to report on life in a segregated society from the other side of the color line.
- Viewable at: https://www.dailymotion.com/video/x7zj7rl

Nothing But a Man
- African American railroad worker marries the school teacher daughter of a local preacher and tries to maintain his self-respect in a racist small town
- One of the first Black feature films with an all-Black cast intended for a diverse audience. Had a hard time finding distribution so has been described as "more famous than familiar"

One Potato, Two Potato
- Study of interracial marriage/custody case in the 1960's

1965

A Patch of Blue
- Tells the friendship between an educated Black man and an illiterate, blind, white, 18-year-old girl who thus cannot see his race
- Film addresses the problems that plague their friendship in a racially divided America
- Viewable at: HBO Max, Apple TV, Amazon Prime Video

1967

Guess Who's Coming to Dinner
- First interracial kiss on film in American cinema
- One of very few films in that era to represent interracial marriage positively (US legalization of interracial marriage happened just six months before the movie came out)
- Viewable at: Vudu, Amazon Prime Video

In the Heat of the Night

- Tells the story of Virgil Tibbs, a Black police detective from Philadelphia, who becomes involved in a murder investigation in a small town in Mississippi, where he is partnered with a racist good-old-boy Southern detective
- Viewable at: YouTube, Apple TV, Amazon Prime Video

To Sir, with Love

- Black engineer who cannot find a job teaches at an inner-city school in the East End of London
- Deals with social, class, and racial issues
- Viewable at: Amazon Prime Video

1968

Planet of the Apes

- An astronaut crew crash-lands on a strange planet in the distant future and stumbles upon a society in which apes have evolved into creatures with human-like intelligence and speech. The apes are the dominant species and the humans are enslaved.
- Good intentions but the choice of monkeys as a stand-in for Black people perpetuated racist tropes
- Played into the issues of skin color hierarchy, making lighter monkeys the more intelligent
- Viewable at: Hulu, Amazon Prime Video

Story of a Three Day Pass

- A Black American soldier is demoted for fraternizing with a white shop clerk in France
- Viewable at: https://www.kanopy.com/product/story-three-day-pass

1969

100 Rifles

- A Native revolutionary robs a bank to buy arms for his oppressed people, but finds himself sought by an American lawman and the Mexican Army
- First interracial sex scene
- Viewable at: Hulu, Starz, Sling TV, Amazon Prime Video

1970

The Great White Hope

- Confronts issues such as racism and man's struggle with the society that surrounds him
- The term, "the great white hope," reflects the racism and segregation of the era in which Jack Johnson fought
- Viewable at: https://www.facebook.com/watch/?v=2527356804197198

The Landlord

- A privileged, selfish, and ignorant white man becomes landlord of an inner-city tenement, unaware that the people he is responsible for are low-income, streetwise residents
- Viewable at: https://www.youtube.com/watch?v=_BZncZK9qk4&ab_channel=MaxDouglas

...tick...tick...tick...

- An African American man elected as the sheriff of a rural county in the American South
- Has become something of a cult classic for its cutting-edge portrayal of racial relations and its tense narrative
- Viewable at: Amazon Prime Video, Apple TV

Watermelon Man

- Tells the story of an extremely bigoted 1960s-era white insurance salesman named Jeff Gerber, who wakes up one morning to find that he has become Black
- Viewable at: Pluto TV, Amazon Prime Video

1971

Brian's Song

- Details the life of Brian Piccolo, a Chicago Bears football player stricken with terminal cancer after turning pro in 1965, told through his friendship with Bears teammate Gale Sayers. Their sharply differing temperaments and racial backgrounds made them unlikely to bond, yet they became close friends and the first interracial roommates in the history of the NFL
- Viewable at: https://www.youtube.com/watch?v=G4SF3h9tvtk&ab_channel=vettshow80

Brother John

- Drama film about an enigmatic African American man who shows up in his Southern hometown every time a relative is about to die. Union agitator or messenger from heaven sent to assess mankind's worthiness of redemption?
- Produced by Sidney Poitier at the height of his fame and power. He also starred.
- Not a critical or box office success
- Viewable at: Vudu, Amazon Prime Video

Shaft (with sequels in 1972 and 1973)

- A private detective named John Shaft is hired by a Harlem mobster to rescue his daughter from the Italian mobsters who kidnapped her
- Gordon Parks became Hollywood's first major Black director
- Viewable at: Sling TV, Hulu, Amazon Prime Video

1972

Buck and the Preacher

- Broke Hollywood Western traditions by casting Black actors as central characters and portraying both tension and solidarity between African Americans and Native Americans in the late 19th century
- Viewable at: Vudu, Amazon Prime Video

Lady Sings the Blues

- Loosely based on the 1956 autobiography of jazz singer Billie Holiday
- Screen debut for Diana Ross
- Viewable at: https://www.youtube.com/watch?v=pScVQQDDyuI&ab_channel=Jazz%26More

Sounder

- Follows the story of a poor African American family struggling in the Deep South during the Great Depression
- Viewable at: Tubi, Sling TV, Hulu, Amazon Prime Video

Blacula

- First Black horror film in blaxploitation era
- An 18th-century African prince named Mamuwalde is turned into a vampire (and later locked in a coffin) by Count Dracula in the Count's castle in Transylvania in the year 1780 after Dracula refused to help Mamuwalde suppress the slave trade

- Viewable at: https://www.youtube.com/watch?v=03P8xytgbU8&ab_channel= BlackintheDayTV

1973

The Spook Who Sat by the Door
- A satire of the civil rights struggle in the United States of the late 1960s and a serious attempt to focus on the issue of Black militancy
- Viewable at: https://www.youtube.com/watch?v=_BynXfREPG8&ab_channel= TheOriginator100

1974

Blazing Saddles
- More than just a satiric comedy/Western or an interracial buddy movie, it is an absurdist comedy that illustrates how senseless racism is through humor.
- It has become a classic but could not be made today in this era of political correctness
- Viewable at: Part 1 - https://www.dailymotion.com/video/x4z3buk

Part 2 - https://www.dailymotion.com/video/x4z3dzp

Conrack
- Based on the 1972 autobiographical book The Water Is Wide by Pat Conroy, who accepts a teaching position on an isolated island in South Carolina, where he finds a class of black students who are not only illiterate, but also wanting for simple personal hygiene. Conroy contradicts the lax institutional standards and exposes his students to a wide range of topics, but those in power do not take kindly to his efforts to overturn their racist policies.
- Viewable at: https://www.youtube.com/watch?v=MyNHgICBFyI&ab_channel= idemoniakoart

---

1975

Deadly Hero
- Neo noir thriller about a violent, trigger-happy detective who is demoted from detective back to patrol duty and has to contend with a hostage situation that he defuses and then kills the Black perp anyway. He convinces the hostage to lie and is hailed a hero. When she finally comes forward with the truth, he terrorizes her.

- Viewable at: https://www.youtube.com/watch?v=I7HRGhuKe50&ab_channel= javiergonzalezpons

1977

Greased Lightning
- Loosely based on the true life story of Wendell Scott, the first African American NASCAR race winner and 2015 NASCAR Hall of Fame inductee
- Viewable at: Part 1 - https://www.dailymotion.com/video/x3iu570

Part 2 - https://www.dailymotion.com/video/x3iu570

1978

The Boys from Brazil
- A Nazi hunter in Paraguay discovers a sinister and bizarre plot to rekindle the Third Reich
- Viewable at: Tubi, Pluto TV, Peacock, Vudu, Amazon Prime Video

1979

I Know Why The Caged Bird Sings
- Traces the life of Maya Angelou from when she and her brother move in with their grandmother to the trauma of being raped as a young girl by one of her mother's boyfriends and the several years of silence that came after the attack
- Viewable at: https://www.youtube.com/watch?v=JG1e7fzsrJQ&ab_channel=reelblack

1981

Crisis At Central High
- Made-for-television movie about the Little Rock Integration Crisis of 1957, based on a draft of the memoir by the same name by former assistant principal Elizabeth Huckaby
- Viewable at: https://www.youtube.com/watch?v=80yRfbz_kxg&ab_channel=reelblack

Ragtime
- A young Black pianist becomes embroiled in the lives of an upper-class white family set among the racial tensions, infidelity, and violence of early 1900s New York City

- Later adapted into a Broadway musical (See 'Theatre' → 'Musical Theatre' → 'Ragtime' for plot summary and significance)
- Viewable at: YouTube, Apple TV, Amazon Prime Video

1982

A House Divided: Denmark Vesey's Rebellion
- Television film about Denmark Vesey, a literate skilled carpenter and former slave who planned a slave rebellion in 1822 in Charleston, South Carolina
- Viewable at: Tubi, Amazon Prime Video

White Dog
- Depicts the struggle of a Black dog trainer named Keys who is trying to retrain a stray dog that is a "white dog"—a dog trained to make vicious attacks upon, and to kill, any Black person
- Serves as a platform to deliver a message against racism as it examines the question of whether racism is a treatable problem or an incurable condition

1984

The Cotton Club
- Surrounds a Harlem jazz club in the 1930s called the Cotton Club
- Viewable at: Pluto TV, Vudu, Amazon Prime Video

Places in the Heart
- In central Texas in the 1930s, a recent widow struggles to survive with two small children, a farm to run, and the unwelcome presence of the Ku Klux Klan. Viewable at: Vudu, Amazon Prime Video

A Soldier's Story
- An African American officer investigates a murder in a racially charged situation in World War II
- Viewable at: Amazon Prime Video

1985

And The Children Shall Lead
- A 12-year-old African American girl and her white friends try to ease increasing racial tensions

- Viewable at: https://www.youtube.com/watch?v=tzIcr1zlZBE&ab_channel= TheeSymphony%27sCultureChannel

The Color Purple
- A Black Southern woman struggles to find her identity after suffering abuse from her father and others over four decades
- See 'Theatre' → 'Musical Theatre' → *'The Color Purple'* for plot summary and significance
- Viewable at: Hulu, HBO Max

1986

Native Son
- In 1940s Chicago, a young Black man takes a job as a chauffeur to a white family, which takes a turn for the worse when he accidentally kills the teenage daughter of the couple and then tries to cover it up.
- Viewable at: https://www.youtube.com/watch?v=MyuchNlmCAw&ab_ channel=reelblack

She's Gotta Have It
- Propelled Spike Lee's rise to fame and made him a successful and bankable African American filmmaker
- Critical and box office success among diverse audiences
- Viewable at: Netflix

Soul Man
- A white law student pretends to be Black in order to qualify for a scholarship
- Viewable at: YouTube, Vudu, Amazon Prime Video

1987

Hollywood Shuffle
- An actor limited to stereotypical roles because of his ethnicity, dreams of making it big as a highly respected performer
- Satirizes the Hollywood film industry and its treatment of African Americans
- Viewable at: https://www.youtube.com/watch?v=CQ8l4372nXg&ab_ channel=YouTubeMovies

1988

Betrayed

- An female FBI agent goes undercover and becomes romantically involved with a Midwest farmer who lives a double life as a white supremacist leader. She must betray the man she loves or the FBI.
- Viewable at: Hulu, Sling TV, Amazon Prime Video

Bird

- Details the troubled life and career of jazz musician Charlie "Bird" Parker
- Viewable at: YouTube, iTunes, Apple TV

Hairspray

- Teenager Tracy Turnblad teaches 1962 Baltimore a thing or two about integration after landing a spot on a local TV dance show
- See 'Theatre' → 'Musical Theatre' → '*Hairspray*' for plot summary and significance
- Viewable at: Tubi, HBO Max

Mississippi Burning

- Two F.B.I. Agents with wildly different styles arrive in Mississippi to investigate the disappearance of three civil rights activists. Loosely based on a true story from the civil rights movement of the 1960s
- Viewable at: Hulu, Amazon Prime Video

School Daze

- A not so popular young man wants to pledge to a popular fraternity at his historically Black college
- Spike Lee's follow up film and a continuation of his exploration of Black life that finds success with diverse audiences
- Viewable at: Showtime

Stand and Deliver

- The true story of Jaime Escalante, a high school teacher who successfully inspired his dropout-prone, inner-city students to learn calculus and prepared them for college
- Viewable at: Hulu, Amazon Prime Video

1989

A Dry White Season

- A white middle class South African suburbanite with no interest in politics agrees to help his Black gardener find his jailed son

- Takes on apartheid
- Viewable at: Tubi

Do the Right Thing

- On the hottest day of the year on a street in the Bedford-Stuyvesant section of Brooklyn, everyone's hate and bigotry smolders and builds until it explodes into violence
- Viewable at: Hulu, Starz, Amazon Prime Video

Driving Miss Daisy

- An old Jewish woman and her African American chauffeur in the American South have a relationship that grows and improves over the years
- Viewable at: Tubi, HBO Max

Glory

- Robert Gould Shaw leads the U.S. Civil War's first all-Black volunteer company, fighting prejudices from both his own Union Army, and the Confederates.
- Won many Academy Awards including Best Actor for Denzel Washington
- Viewable at: https://www.youtube.com/watch?v=2LP4tPnCZt4&ab_channel=HoangDinhNgoc

Lean on Me

- True story of the dedicated but tyrannical Joe Clark who is appointed the principal of a decaying inner-city school he is determined to improve by any and all means
- Viewable at: HBO Max

My Past Is My Own

- Centered on a sit-in in the early 1960s at a racially segregated lunch counter in the Southern United States

1990

Come See the Paradise

- The passionate romance between an Irish-American man and a Japanese-American woman is threatened when the Pearl Harbor attacks happen and the woman is forced into a prison camp because of her ethnicity
- Viewable at: YouTube, iTunes, Apple TV, Amazon Prime Video

The Long Walk Home

- Two women, Black and white, in 1955 Montgomery Alabama, must decide what they are going to do in response to the famous bus boycott led by Martin Luther King

- Viewable at: Tubi, Vudu, Pluto TV, Amazon Prime Video

Murder In Mississippi

- In 1964, members of the Ku Klux Klan murdered three Civil Rights workers who had traveled to the South to encourage African American voter registration. The film examines the last three weeks in the lives of the slain activists.
- Viewable at: https://www.youtube.com/watch?v=-k5YTDlh7Wo&ab_channel= TheBlackestPanther

Q & A

- Dirty cop, Mike Brennan, thinks he got away with killing a Puerto Rican man, but during a routine Q&A, the righteous assistant DA finds a clue that sets them both on a collision course
- Police brutality towards minorities comes into play
- Viewable at: YouTube, iTunes, Apple TV, Amazon Prime Video

Paris Is Burning

- A documentary about New York's drag scene in the 1980s, focusing on balls, voguing and the ambitions and dreams of those who gave the era its warmth and vitality
- First instance in which ball culture is documented for mainstream consumption
- Viewable at: https://www.youtube.com/watch?v=mBVBipOl76Q&ab_channel= FelipeCavalcante

1991

Brother Future

- A young street rapper is transported back in time to the pre-Civil War South, where he finds himself in the middle of a slave revolt.
- Viewable at: Tubi, Vudu, Amazon Prime Video

Daughters of the Dust

- Languid look at the Gullah culture of the sea islands off the coast of South Carolina and Georgia where African folk-ways were maintained well into the 20th Century and was one of the last bastions of these mores in America
- First film directed by a Black woman to get national distribution
- Viewable at: HBO Max, Amazon Prime Video

Fried Green Tomatoes

- A housewife who is unhappy with her life befriends an old lady in a nursing home and is enthralled by the tales she tells of people she used to know

- Deals with the segregation era and class divides based on race
- Viewable at: Peacock

Jungle Fever

- Friends and family of a married Black architect react in different ways to his affair with an Italian secretary

Mississippi Masala

- Follows an Indian family that is expelled from Idi Amin's Uganda in 1972 and immigrates to Mississippi
- Interracial romance between Indian American and African American
- Directed by Mira Nair, an Indian woman
- Viewable at: https://www.youtube.com/watch?v=Dp6KGCwA1iY&ab_channel= KajolGiri

1992

Love Field

- Devastated by President Kennedy's assassination, Dallas-based hairstylist Lurene Hallett boards a bus for the Washington funeral where she meets a friendly black man and his young daughter, but after a series of strange events the three of them are pursued by the police, the FBI and some brutal racists
- Viewable at: iTunes, Vudu, Apple TV, Amazon Prime Video

Malcolm X

- Biographical epic of the controversial and influential Black Nationalist leader, from his early life and career as a small-time gangster, to his ministry as a member of the Nation of Islam
- Viewable at: Hulu, HBO Max

The Power of One

- An English boy, living in Africa during World War II, through his boxing prowess, becomes a symbol of hope, in a time of war
- Viewable at: iTunes, YouTube, Apple TV, Amazon Prime Video

Sarafina!

- Based on the stage musical, South African teenagers fight against apartheid in the Soweto Uprising
- Viewable at: iTunes, Apple TV, Amazon Prime Video

School Ties

- Set in the 1950s, a star-quarterback is given an opportunity to attend an elite preparatory school but must conceal the fact that he is Jewish
- Viewable at: Pluto TV, Amazon Prime Video, Paramount+

Zebrahead

- A white, hip-hop loving teen falls in love with a Black girl
- Viewable at: https://www.youtube.com/watch?v=oU6wIkgygWg&ab_channel=Chiraqology%E2%80%A2

1993

A Bronx Tale

- Tells the coming of age story of an Italian-American boy, Calogero, who, after encountering a local Mafia boss, is torn between the temptations of organized crime and the values of his honest, hardworking father, as well as racial tensions in his community
- Viewable at: YouTube, Vudu, Amazon Prime Video

Class of '61

- Three West Point 1861 generation cadets and friends go on opposite sides after the breakout of The Civil War, with tragic consequences
- Viewable at:

   Part 1 - https://www.youtube.com/watch?v=Bl2imLgV7V0&ab_channel=LionHeart FilmWorks

   Part 2 - https://www.youtube.com/watch?v=bURtNCB4EVg&ab_channel=LionHeart FilmWorks

   Part 3 - https://www.youtube.com/watch?v=UPsyc4ky8a8&ab_channel=LionHeart FilmWorks

The Ernest Green Story

- Follows the story of Ernest Green, one of the Little Rock Nine who were the first Black individuals to integrate into an all white school
- Viewable at: https://www.youtube.com/watch?v=UPsyc4ky8a8&ab_channel=LionHeartFilmWorks

Menace II Society

- A young street hustler attempts to escape the rigors and temptations of the ghetto in a quest for a better life

- Gained notoriety for its scenes of violence, profanity, drug-related content, and its realistic portrayal of urban violence
- Viewable at: HBO Max

The Meteor Man

- A high school teacher from a troubled inner city Washington D.C. neighborhood becomes a super-powered hero and takes on the gang that has been terrorizing his streets
- First Black superhero film

Sankofa

- A self-absorbed Black American fashion model on a photo shoot in Africa is spiritually transported back to a plantation in the West Indies where she experiences first-hand the physical and psychic horrors of chattel slavery

Schindler's List

- In German-occupied Poland during World War II, industrialist Oskar Schindler gradually becomes concerned for his Jewish workforce after witnessing their persecution by the Nazis
- Viewable at: YouTube, iTunes, Apple TV, Vudu, Amazon Prime Video

1994

Assault at West Point: The Court-Martial of Johnson Whittaker

- The story of Johnson Whittaker, one of the first African American cadets admitted to West Point, who was tied down and beaten by his fellow cadets and then court-martialed on the grounds that he staged his own assault to avoid taking a philosophy exam
- Viewable at: https://www.youtube.com/watch?v=oZmuaP_TX7w&ab_channel=Lion HeartFilmWorks

Corrina, Corrina

- A widower hires a kindly Black housekeeper/nanny to care for his seven-year-old daughter
- Viewable at: Tubi

The Shawshank Redemption

- Tells the story of banker Andy Dufresne who is sentenced to life in Shawshank State Penitentiary for the murders of his wife and her lover, despite his claims of innocence. Over the following two decades, he befriends a Black prisoner, contraband smuggler Ellis "Red" Redding and becomes instrumental in a money-laundering operation led by the prison warden. Explores prison brutality

- Viewable at: https://www.youtube.com/watch?v=DyKrAnBMgtA&ab_channel= JitenderKumar

Whitewash

- An animated short that tells the story of a little Black girl's first encounter with mindless racism when she is set upon by a racist gang that spray paints her face white.
- Viewable at: YouTube, Amazon Prime Video

1995

Cry, the Beloved Country

- Set in pre-apartheid South Africa, this film tells the story of a church minister who discovers that his son has been arrested for the murder of a white man, whose father supports apartheid. However, when the two meet, they come to unexpected understandings about their sons and their own humanity.
- Viewable at: Crackle

High Lonesome

- A poor Black sharecropper strikes up an unlikely friendship with a hostile young white boy, but their budding friendship is threatened by a brutal red-neck sheriff
- Viewable at: https://www.youtube.com/watch?v=CkKRQNlJ3nM&ab_ channel=VictorLaurant

Higher Learning

- People from all different walks of life, encounter racial tension, rape, responsibility, and the meaning of an education on a university campus
- Viewable at: Hulu, Starz, Amazon Prime Video

Jefferson In Paris

- Widower Thomas Jefferson has a beautiful young slave girl, Sally Hemmings, accompany his daughter to France and has an alleged affair with her resulting in kids
- Viewable at: iTunes

The Journey of August King

- On his journey home from selling his produce and purchasing goods he will need for the coming year, August King comes upon a runaway slave and must decide to violate the law by helping her to freedom or leave her to be hunted down and, ultimately, returned to her slave owner

- Viewable at: Google Play, Vudu, Amazon Prime Video

Losing Isaiah

- The Black biological mother and white adoptive mother of a young boy are involved in a bitter, controversial custody battle
- Viewable at: Amazon Prime Video

Pocahontas

- An English soldier and the daughter of an Algonquin chief share a romance when English colonists invade seventeenth century Virginia
- An example of the romanticization of the historical relationship that European immigrants fostered with the Natives
- Viewable at: Disney+

The Tuskegee Airmen

- The true story of how a group of African American pilots overcame racist opposition to become one of the finest US fighter groups in World War II
- Viewable at: HBO Max

The Walking Dead

- Set in 1972 Vietnam, a small group of United States Marines relive flashbacks of their lives prior to serving in the military while being left to survive behind enemy lines
- Deals with anti-Asian propaganda that was sweeping the nation at the time
- Viewable at: Peacock

White Man's Burden

- In an alternative America where African Americans and White Americans have reversed cultural roles, a white factory worker kidnaps a Black factory owner for dismissing him over perceived disdain

---

1996

A Family Thing

- When head of an Arkansas equipment rental outfit Earl Pilcher, Jr.'s mother dies, leaving a letter explaining he's not her natural son but the son of a Black woman who died in childbirth, Earl ventures to Chicago to meet her. Initially he receives a cold welcome until his birth mother's sister, Aunt T., an aged and blind matriarch, takes Earl in tow and insists that the family open up to him

- Viewable at: Hulu, Amazon Prime Video

The Chamber

- A young man fresh out of law school tries to win a reprieve for his racist grandfather who is on death row
- Viewable at: Hulu, Starz, Amazon Prime Video

Get On The Bus

- A disparate group of African American men travel by bus to Washington, DC for the Million Man March
- Viewable at: Tubi

Ghosts of Mississippi

- A Mississippi district attorney and the widow of Medgar Evers struggle to finally bring a white racist to justice for the 1963 murder of the civil rights leader
- Viewable at: Tubi, Amazon Prime Video

The Hunchback of Notre Dame

- A bell-ringer with a physical deformity must assert his independence from a vicious government minister in order to help his friend, a gypsy dancer
- Implies, according to Mark Pinsky, a "condemnation of abortion, euthanasia, and racism, and [a] moral resistance to genocide"
- Viewable at: Disney+

Mr. and Mrs. Loving

- A moving and ultimately uplifting true story about miscegenation laws and the first case that made it to the Supreme Court and won
- Viewable at: Pluto TV, Vudu, Amazon Prime Video

Nightjohn

- Follows the story of a 12 year-old slave girl named Sarny whose life is changed when she is taught how to read by a fellow slave
- Viewable at: Amazon Prime Video

Soul Of The Game

- Black baseball greats, Satchel Paige and Josh Gibson, vie to be the first Black major leaguer, only to see the outspoken rookie, Jackie Robinson, be chosen
- Viewable at: https://www.youtube.com/watch?v=LiDULxPh0hU&ab_channel= NegroLeagueHistory

A Time To Kill

- In Canton, Mississippi, a fearless young lawyer and his assistant defend a Black man accused of murdering two white men who raped his ten-year-old daughter, inciting violent retribution and revenge from the Ku Klux Klan
- Viewable at: Tubi, HBO Max

The Watermelon Woman

- A young Black lesbian filmmaker probes into the life of The Watermelon Woman, a 1930s Black actress who played 'mammy' archetypes
- First Black lesbian film
- Viewable at: Showtime, Hulu, Amazon Prime Video

1997

Amistad

- The revolt of Mende captives aboard a Spanish owned ship causes a major controversy in the United States when the ship is captured off the coast of Long Island. The courts must decide whether the Mende are slaves or legally free.
- Black story told primarily by whites behind the camera
- Viewable at: HBO Max

Buffalo Soldiers

- Fact based story about the all-Black US Cavalry Troop H which protected the Western territories in post Civil War times
- Examines the racial tensions that existed between the Black soldiers and some of the white soldiers and the truths about the native invaders
- Viewable at: Apple TV, Amazon Prime Video

Miss Evers' Boys

- The true story of the U.S. Government's 1932 Tuskegee Syphilis Experiment, in which a group of Black test subjects were allowed to die, despite a cure having been developed
- Viewable at: HBO Max

Rosewood

- A dramatization of a horrific 1923 racist lynch mob attack on an African American community
- Viewable at: YouTube, iTunes, Google Play, Apple TV, Amazon Prime Video

1998

American History X

- A former neo-nazi skinhead tries to prevent his younger brother from going down the same wrong path that he did
- Viewable at: Tubi

Apt Pupil

- A boy blackmails his neighbor after suspecting him to be a Nazi war criminal
- Viewable at: Hulu, Starz, Amazon Prime Video

Beloved

- Based on the book by Toni Morrison, in which a slave is visited by the spirit of a mysterious young woman
- Viewable at: Amazon Prime Video

Ruby Bridges

- When six-year-old Ruby is chosen to be the first African American to integrate her local elementary school, she is subjected to the true ugliness of racism for the first time
- Viewable at: Disney+

The Way Home: Women Talk about Race in America

- Over the course of eight months, sixty-four women representing a cross-section of cultures (Indigenous, African American, Arab/Middle Eastern, Asian, European-American, Jewish, Latina, and Multiracial) came together to share their experience of racism in America
- Viewable at: https://vimeo.com/ondemand/thewayhome

1999

A Lesson Before Dying

- In the 1940s South, an African American man is wrongly accused of the killing of a white store owner, and, in his defense, his white attorney equates him with a lowly hog, to indicate that he didn't have the sense to know what he was doing
- Viewable at: https://www.youtube.com/watch?v=2FVoZ-C70ic&ab_channel=Jesuswept. Movies2

Crazy in Alabama

- An abused wife heads to California to become a movie star while her nephew back in Alabama has to deal with a racially-motivated murder involving a corrupt sheriff

- Viewable at: Vudu, Amazon Prime Video

The Green Mile

- The lives of guards on Death Row are affected by one of their charges: a Black man accused of child murder and rape, yet who has a mysterious gift
- Viewable at: Cinemax

Having Our Say: The Delany Sisters' First 100 Years

- Tells the story of Sadie and Bessie Delany, two African American (they preferred "colored") daughters of the first African American Episcopal bishop, who was born a slave, and a woman with a multi-racial background, who both lived past the age of 100
- Viewable at: Vudu, Amazon Prime Video

The Hurricane

- The story of Rubin 'Hurricane' Carter, a boxer wrongly imprisoned for murder, and the people who aided in his fight to prove his innocence
- Viewable at: HBO Max

Introducing Dorothy Dandridge

- Dorothy Dandridge's way to fame and fortune as a dancer, singer and actress
- Viewable at: HBO Max, Hulu, Amazon Prime Video

The Secret Path

- A drama about a young, neglected white girl in the rural South who, with the help of a Black couple, finds the solace and nurturing needed to transform her downtrodden life
- Viewable at: Tubi, Amazon Prime Video

Selma, Lord, Selma

- In 1965 Alabama, an 11 year old girl is touched by a speech by Martin Luther King, Jr. and becomes a devout follower, but her resolution is tested when she joins others in the famed march from Selma to Montgomery
- Viewable at: https://www.youtube.com/watch?v=Mh9p8TiNG2c&ab_channel=waen-tvatlanta

Snow Falling On Cedars

- A Japanese-American fisherman is accused of killing his neighbor at sea
- Viewable at: YouTube, iTunes, Google Play, Apple TV, Amazon Prime Video

2000

A Storm in Summer

- An old Jewish shop owner Mr. Shaddick suddenly finds himself responsible for a little Black boy named Herman Washington trying to escape the chaos of Harlem as part of a sponsorship program
- Viewable at: https://www.youtube.com/watch?v=RDdN-tcYLGQ&ab_channel= TheeSymphony%27sCultureChannel

Bamboozled

- A frustrated African American TV writer proposes a blackface minstrel show in protest, but to his chagrin it becomes a hit
- Viewable at: Amazon Prime Video

The Color of Friendship

- A white South African girl finds herself in a difficult situation when she is sent to spend a term with a Black family in America
- Viewable at: Disney+

Finding Forrester

- Black teenager Jamal Wallace is invited to attend a prestigious private high school and befriends reclusive writer William Forrester through whom he refines his talent for writing and comes to terms with his identity
- Viewable at: Hulu, Starz, Amazon Prime Video

Freedom Song

- A father and son clash regarding how to deal with the racism they encounter in the 1960s, in Mississippi, before Blacks were allowed to vote, and did sit ins at White establishments

Men of Honor

- The story of Carl Brashear, the first African American U.S. Navy Diver, and the man who trained him
- Viewable at: YouTube, Amazon Prime Video

Remember the Titans

- The true story of a newly appointed African American coach and his high school team on their first season as a racially integrated unit
- Viewable at: Disney+

Two Family House
- A dreamer finds that his wife and friends are binding him to his mediocre existence. Racial prejudice that arises when a mixed race baby is born holds the key to his escape.
- Viewable at: iTunes

2001

The Believer
- A young Jewish man develops a fiercely antisemitic philosophy
- Based on the factual story of a K.K.K. member in the 1960s who was revealed to be Jewish by a New York Times reporter
- Viewable at: Tubi, Amazon Prime Video

Bojangles
- The life of Bill "Bojangles" Robinson, African American tap-dancing star of stage and screen
- Viewable at: Tubi

Boycott
- Black Americans boycott the public buses during the 1950s civil rights movement
- Viewable at: HBO Max

Feast Of All Saints
- Depicts the gens de couleur libre, or the Free People of Colour, a dazzling yet damned class in the 18ᵗʰ and 19ᵗʰ century. A biracial man is caught between the world of white privilege and Black oppression in 19ᵗʰ century New Orleans.

Focus
- In the waning months of World War II, a man and his wife are mistakenly identified as Jews by their antisemitic Brooklyn neighbors. Suddenly the victims of religious and racial persecution, the couple becomes aligned with a local Jewish immigrant in a struggle for dignity and survival.
- Viewable at: YouTube, iTunes, Google Play, Vudu, Amazon Prime Video

Monster's Ball
- After a family tragedy, a racist prison guard re-examines his attitudes while falling in love with the African American wife of the last prisoner he executed
- Viewable at: Amazon Prime Video

Ruby's Bucket of Blood
- A Louisiana juke joint owner loses her star entertainer and hires a white singer to fill in
- Viewable at: Tubi

2002

10,000 Black Men Named George
- Union activist Asa Philip Randolph's efforts to organize the Black porters of the Pullman Rail Company in 1920s America
- Viewable at: https://www.youtube.com/watch?v=RciZm3_tm8E&ab_channel=reelblack

The Bronze Screen: 100 Years of the Latino Image in American Cinema
- Documentary about the presence of Latin American culture and actors in American movies
- Viewable at: Amazon Prime Video

Far from Heaven
- In 1950s Connecticut, a housewife faces a marital crisis and mounting racial tensions in the outside world
- Viewable at: Showtime

Hart's War
- A law student becomes a lieutenant during World War II, is captured and asked to defend a Black prisoner of war falsely accused of murder
- Viewable at: YouTube, Tubi, Pluto TV, Showtime, Amazon Prime Video

Keep The Faith, Baby
- New Yorker Adam Clayton Powell Jr. becomes a congressman and condemns all forms of segregation and discrimination
- Viewable at: https://www.youtube.com/watch?v=QkIZdGhR6ZA&ab_channel=reelblack

The Pianist
- A Polish Jewish musician struggles to survive the destruction of the Warsaw ghetto of World War II
- Viewable at: Netflix

Sins of the Father
- Recounts the story of Bobby Frank Cherry, who participated in the infamous 1963 bombing of a Birmingham, Ala., church that left four Black girls dead

The Rosa Parks Story
- A seamstress recalls events leading to her act of peaceful defiance that prompted the 1955 bus boycott in Montgomery, Alabama
- Viewable at: Amazon Prime Video

2003

Deacons For Defense
- Loosely based on the activities of the Deacons for Defense and Justice in 1965 in Bogalusa, Louisiana
- Viewable at: Tubi

Light in the Shadows
- A frank dialogue about race among two white women and several women of color
- Viewable at: https://vimeo.com/ondemand/lightintheshadows

2004

Crash
- Los Angeles citizens with vastly separate lives collide in interweaving stories of race, loss, and redemption
- Viewable at: Amazon Prime Video, YouTube

A Day Without a Mexican
- When a mysterious fog surrounds the boundaries of California, there is a communication breakdown and all the Mexicans disappear, affecting the economy and the state stops working missing the Mexican workers and dwellers

Harold & Kumar Go to White Castle
- A Korean-American office worker and his Indian-American stoner friend embark on a quest to satisfy their desire for White Castle burgers
- Viewable at: Hulu, Starz, Amazon Prime Video

Hotel Rwanda
- Paul Rusesabagina, a hotel manager, houses over a thousand Tutsi refugees during their struggle against the Hutu militia in Rwanda, Africa
- Viewable at: YouTube, Tubi, Pluto TV, Amazon Prime Video

Ray

- The story of the life and career of the legendary rhythm and blues musician Ray Charles, from his humble beginnings in the South, where he went blind at age seven, to his meteoric rise to stardom during the 1950s and 1960s
- Viewable at: HBO Max

Something The Lord Made

- A dramatization of the true relationship between heart surgery pioneers Alfred Blalock and Vivien Thomas. Blaylock was white and Thomas was Black.
- Viewable at: HBO Max

White Chicks

- Two disgraced Black FBI agents go way undercover as blonde white women in an effort to solve a kidnapping plot. In using whiteface, it punches back at blackface.
- Viewable at: Vudu, Amazon Prime Video

2005

500 Years Later

- Told from the vantage-point of those whom history has sought to silence by examining the collective atrocities that uprooted Africans from their culture and homeland
- Viewable at: YouTube, iTunes, Apple TV, Google Play, Amazon Prime Video

Animal

- A notorious gangster nicknamed "Animal" must reconcile his past in order to make a future for his criminally-minded son. He steps out of the vicious cycle destroying Black communities when he immerses himself in the writings of Malcolm X while in prison.
- Viewable at: Tubi, Pluto TV, Peacock, Vudu, Amazon Prime Video

Guess Who

- A young Black woman, Theresa, brings her boyfriend, Simon, home to meet her parents and surprise them with the news of their engagement. Another surprise: Simon is white.
- Viewable at: Hulu, Amazon Prime Video

Manderlay

- A story of slavery, set in the southern U.S. in the 1930s

2006

Americanese
- Long after their breakup, Chinese American Raymond Ding and Amerasian Aurora Crane struggle to let go

Borat: Cultural Learnings of America for Make Benefit Glorious Nation of Kazakhstan
- Kazakh TV talking head Borat is dispatched to the United States to report on the greatest country in the world. With a documentary crew in tow, Borat becomes more interested in locating and marrying Pamela Anderson.
- Deals with race and the superiority complex of the American populace
- Viewable at: YouTube, Hulu, Starz, Amazon Prime Video

Flags of Our Fathers
- The life stories of the six men who raised the flag at the Battle of Iwo Jima, with the story of Ira Hayes, a Native, as a standout because of the racism he experienced. The cost of war on all who participate.
- Viewable at: HBO Max

Glory Road
- In 1966, Texas Western coach Don Haskins led the first all-Black starting line-up for a college basketball team to the NCAA national championship
- Viewable at: Disney+, Cinemax

Milk
- The story of Harvey Milk and his struggles as an American gay activist who fought for gay rights and became California's first openly gay elected official before he was assassinated
- Viewable at: https://www.facebook.com/watch/?v=778465776010918

Mirrors of Privilege: Making Whiteness Visible
- Reveals what is often required to move through the stages of denial, defensiveness, guilt, fear, and shame into making a solid commitment to ending racial injustice
- Viewable at: https://vimeo.com/ondemand/mirrorsofprivilege

Something New
- Kenya McQueen, a Black accountant finds love in the most unexpected place when she agrees to go on a blind date with Brian Kelly, a free-spirited white landscape architect
- Viewable at: Peacock

2007

Freedom Writers

- A young teacher inspires her class of at-risk students to learn tolerance, apply themselves and pursue education beyond high school
- Viewable at: Paramount+, YouTube

The Great Debaters

- A drama based on the true story of Melvin B. Tolson, a professor at Wiley College Texas, who inspired students to form the school's first debate team (something nearly unheard of for a predominantly Black institution), which went on to challenge Harvard in the national championship
- Viewable at: Amazon Prime Video

Hairspray

- Movie musical adaptation of *Hairspray* (1988)
- See 'Theatre' → 'Musical Theatre' → *'Hairspray'* for plot summary and significance
- Viewable at: HBO Max

Pride

- The determined Jim Ellis starts a swim team for troubled teens at the Philadelphia Department of Recreation
- Viewable at: Peacock

Talk To Me

- The story of Washington D.C. radio personality Ralph "Petey" Greene, an ex-con who became a popular talk show host and community activist in the 1960s
- Viewable at: Hulu, YouTube

2008

Beautiful Me(s): Finding Our Revolutionary Selves

- A group of predominantly African American students travel from the Ivy League to the rebel state of Cuba

The Express: The Ernie Davis Story

- A drama based on the life of college football hero Ernie Davis, the first African American to win the Heisman Trophy
- Viewable at: Hulu, Starz, Amazon Prime Video

Gospel Hill

- A former Sheriff of the Southern town dealing with past sins, and a former civil rights worker, withdrawn since the martyrdom of his brother thirty years before, confront a threat to their town
- Viewable at: iTunes

Lakeview Terrace

- Based on a true story, a troubled and racist African American L.A.P.D. Officer will stop at nothing to force out a friendly interracial couple who just moved in next door to him
- Viewable at: Hulu, iTunes, TNT, TBS

A Raisin in the Sun

- Made-for-television remake of the 1961 film based on the play by Lorraine Hansberry
- An African American family struggles with poverty, racism, and inner conflict as they strive for a better way of life
- Viewable at: https://www.youtube.com/watch?v=uZmCR1k2s6o&ab_channel= KnowledgeBuilder

The Secret Life of Bees

- In 1964, a white teenage girl in search of the truth about her mother runs away to a small town in South Carolina and finds a family of independent Black women who can connect her to her past
- Viewable at: YouTube, Peacock, Hulu, Cinemax, Amazon Prime Video

---

2009

The Blind Side

- The story of Michael Oher, a homeless and traumatized boy who became an All-American football player and first-round NFL draft pick with the help of a caring white woman and her family
- Viewable at: HBO Max

Gran Torino

- Disgruntled Korean War veteran Walt Kowalski sets out to reform his neighbor, Thao Lor, a Hmong teenager who tried to steal Kowalski's prized possession: a 1972 Gran Torino

Inglourious Basterds
- In Nazi-occupied France during World War II, a plan to assassinate Nazi leaders by a group of Jewish U.S. soldiers coincides with a theatre owner's vengeful plans for the same
- Viewable at: YouTube, iTunes, Apple TV, Google Play, Amazon Prime Video

Invictus
- Nelson Mandela, in his first term as President of South Africa, initiates a unique venture to unite the Apartheid-torn land: enlist the national rugby team, which was integrated, on a mission to win the 1995 Rugby World Cup
- Viewable at: Netflix, YouTube

The Princess and The Frog
- Disney introduces the first African American princess, Tiana
- A waitress, desperate to fulfill her dreams as a restaurant owner, is set on a journey to turn a frog prince back into a human being, but she instead turns into a frog herself after she kisses him
- Viewable at: Disney+, Netflix, iTunes

Reel Injun
- Documentary that tells the history of the depiction of Native Americans in Hollywood films
- Viewable at: https://www.youtube.com/watch?v=A8CE0S45A2E&ab_channel= TIFFTalks

---

2010

Blood Done Sign My Name
- A drama based on a true story, in which a Black Vietnam-era veteran is allegedly murdered by a local white businessman, who is later exonerated
- Viewable at: YouTube, Amazon Prime Video

For Colored Girls
- Each of the women portray one of the characters represented in the collection of twenty poems, revealing different issues that impact women in general and women of color in particular
- Viewable at: YouTube, iTunes, Apple TV, Google Play, Amazon Prime Video

Frankie and Alice

- A drama centered on a Black go-go dancer with multiple personality disorder who struggles to remain her true self and begins working with a psychotherapist to uncover the mystery of the inner ghosts that haunt her, one of them a Southern white racist woman.
- Viewable at: YouTube, Amazon Prime Video

Night Catches Us

- In 1976, complex political and emotional forces are set in motion when a young man returns to the race-torn Philadelphia neighborhood where he came of age during the Black Power movement
- Viewable at: Tubi, Vudu, Pluto TV, Crackle

2011

The Help

- An aspiring author during the civil rights movement of the 1960s decides to write a book detailing the African American maids' point of view on the white families for which they work, and the hardships they go through on a daily basis
- Both the book and the film were criticized for employing the trope of white saviorism
- Viewable at: iTunes, Netflix

Hidden Colors

- Hidden Colors is a documentary about the real and untold history of people of color around the globe that discusses some of the reasons the contributions of African and aboriginal people have been left out of the pages of history
- Viewable at: iTunes, Apple TV

Winnie Mandela

- A drama that chronicles the life of Winnie Mandela from her childhood through her marriage and her husband's incarceration
- Viewable at: YouTube, Google Play, Vudu, Amazon Prime Video

2012

Cloud Atlas

- An exploration of how the actions of individual lives impact one another in the past, present and future, as one soul is shaped from a killer into a hero, and an act of kindness ripples across centuries to inspire a revolution. One of the intertwining plots involves an attorney who harbors a fleeing slave on a voyage from the Pacific Islands in 1849.

- Viewable at: Tubi, iTunes

Cracking the Codes: The System of Racial Inequity

- Asks America to talk about the causes and consequences of systemic inequity
- Viewable at: https://vimeo.com/ondemand/crackingthecodes

Django Unchained

- With the help of a German bounty-hunter, a freed slave sets out to rescue his wife from a brutal plantation-owner in Mississippi
- Viewable at: https://www.youtube.com/watch?v=HKbEC3UyKjY&ab_channel= AngryPopCorn

Lincoln

- As the American Civil War continues to rage, America's president struggles with continuing carnage on the battlefield as he fights with many inside his own cabinet on the decision to emancipate the slaves
- Viewable at: HBO Max, iTunes

The Paperboy

- A reporter returns to his Florida hometown to investigate a case involving a death row inmate who was convicted of murdering a racist lawman
- Viewable at: Tubi, Pluto TV, Peacock, Vudu, Crackle, Amazon Prime Video

2013

12 Years a Slave

- In the antebellum United States, Solomon Northup, a free Black man from upstate New York, is abducted and sold into slavery
- Viewable at: YouTube, Hulu

42

- In 1947, Jackie Robinson becomes the first African American to play in Major League Baseball in the modern era when he was signed by the Brooklyn Dodgers and faces considerable racism in the process
- Viewable at: HBO Max, YouTube

Betty and Coretta

- The widows of Martin Luther King and Malcolm X and how they carry on as single mothers after the assassination of their husbands

- Viewable at: Lifetime Movie Club, iTunes

The Butler

- As Cecil Gaines serves eight presidents during his tenure as a butler at the White House, the civil rights movement, Vietnam, and other major events affect this man's life, family, and American society
- Viewable at: YouTube, Netflix

Fruitvale Station

- The story of Oscar Grant III, a young Black man who was killed in 2009 by BART police officer Johannes Mehserle at the Fruitvale district station of the Bay Area Rapid Transit (BART) system in Oakland
- Viewable at: YouTube, Netflix

InAPPropriate Comedy

- In this comedy film, a computer tablet full of the world's most hilariously offensive apps breaks through the borders of political correctness, stirring up cultural anarchy
- Viewable at: iTunes, Tubi

Mandela: Long Walk to Freedom

- A chronicle of Nelson Mandela's life journey from his childhood in a rural village through to his inauguration as the first democratically elected president of South Africa
- Viewable at: YouTube

Savannah

- Drama about the friendship between an Oxford-educated Southerner and a former Black slave in turn-of-the-century Savannah
- Viewable at: Vudu, Amazon Prime Video

The Retrieval

- On the outskirts of the U.S. Civil War, a boy is sent north by his bounty hunter gang to retrieve a wanted man
- Viewable at: Vudu

Tula: The Revolt

- The story of a man who stood up against his oppressors leading his people in a peaceful march for freedom, equality and brotherhood
- Viewable at: Tubi, Amazon Prime Video

2014

Freedom
- The film tells two stories in parallel. The first is the pre-Civil War escape of a Black family from slavery in Virginia to freedom in Canada, helped by the Underground Railroad, devout Quakers, and Frederick Douglass. The second story is the travel of an ancestor from Africa to a British colony in the New World.
- Viewable at: Tubi, Amazon Prime Video

The Gabby Douglas Story
- The story of the international gymnastics phenomenon who overcame overwhelming odds to become the first African American ever to be named Individual All-Around Champion in artistic gymnastics at the Olympic Games
- Viewable at: Vudu, Amazon Prime Video

Get On Up
- A chronicle of James Brown's rise from extreme poverty to become one of the most influential musicians in history
- Viewable at: YouTube, Netflix

Selma
- A chronicle of Dr. Martin Luther King, Jr.'s campaign to secure equal voting rights via an epic march from Selma to Montgomery, Alabama, in 1965
- Viewable at: Hulu, YouTube

2015

Bessie
- The story of legendary blues performer Bessie Smith, who rose to fame during the 1920s and '30s
- Viewable at: HBO Max, iTunes

The Man Who Knew Infinity
- The story of the life and academic career of the pioneer Indian mathematician, Srinivasa Ramanujan, and his friendship with his mentor, Professor G.H. Hardy
- Viewable at: YouTube, Amazon Prime Video

Straight Outta Compton

- The rap group NWA emerges from the mean streets of Compton in Los Angeles, California, in the mid-1980s and revolutionizes Hip Hop culture with their music and tales about life in the hood
- Viewable at: YouTube, Hulu, Amazon Prime Video

What Happened Miss Simone

- A documentary about the life and legend of Nina Simone, an American singer, pianist, and civil rights activist labeled the "High Priestess of Soul"
- Viewable at: iTunes, Netflix

2016

All The Way

- Lyndon B. Johnson becomes the President of the United States in the chaotic aftermath of John F. Kennedy's assassination and spends his first year in office fighting to pass the Civil Rights Act
- Viewable at: YouTube, HBO Max

An American Girl Story: Melody 1963 - Love Has to Win

- Set in Detroit during the Civil Rights Movement, "An American Girl Story - Melody 1963: Love Has to Win" examines the joyful life and troubled times of an irrepressible 10-year-old African American girl whose vivid imagination and creativity reinforce her optimism

The Birth of a Nation

- Nat Turner, a literate slave and preacher in the antebellum South, orchestrates an uprising
- Controversy surrounding the filmmaker made the film less successful
- Viewable at: YouTube, Google Play, Apple TV, Vudu, Amazon Prime Video

Free State of Jones

- A disillusioned Confederate army deserter returns to Mississippi and leads a militia of fellow deserters and women in an uprising against the corrupt local Confederate government
- Viewable at: YouTube, Netflix

Hidden Figures

- The true story of a team of female African American mathematicians who served a vital role in NASA during the early years of the U.S. space program but were given no credit for their roles

- Viewable at: YouTube, Disney+

I Am Not Your Negro

- Writer James Baldwin tells the story of race in modern America with his unfinished novel, Remember This House
- Viewable at: YouTube, Tubi, Pluto TV, Vudu, Netflix, Amazon Prime Video

LBJ

- Lyndon B. Johnson aligns himself with John F. Kennedy, rises to the Presidency, and deals with the civil rights struggles of the 1960s
- Viewable at: YouTube, Google Play, Vudu, Amazon Prime Video

Loving

- The story of Richard and Mildred Loving, a couple whose arrest for interracial marriage in 1960s Virginia began a legal battle that would end with the Supreme Court's historic 1967 decision
- Viewable at: Netflix, YouTube, Amazon Prime Video

Moonlight

- First Black LGBTQ+ film to win an Academy Award for best picture
- A young African American man grapples with his identity and sexuality while experiencing the everyday struggles of childhood, adolescence, and burgeoning adulthood
- Viewable at: Showtime, Youtube

The North Star

- The story of Benjamin "Big Ben" Jones and Moses Hopkins, two slaves who escaped from a Virginia plantation and made their way to freedom in Buckingham, Pennsylvania in 1849

Race

- Jesse Owens' quest to become the greatest track and field athlete in history thrusts him onto the world stage of the 1936 Olympics, where he faces off against Adolf Hitler's vision of Aryan supremacy
- Viewable at: YouTube, Google Play, Apple TV, Vudu, Amazon Prime Video

Zootopia

- In a city of anthropomorphic animals, a rookie bunny cop and a cynical con artist fox must work together to uncover a conspiracy
- Central message of the film aims to help kids confront issues of stereotypes and prejudice, favoring nurture over nature
- Viewable at: Disney+, iTunes

2017

Detroit

- Fact-based drama set during the 1967 Detroit riots in which a group of rogue police officers respond to a complaint with retribution against African Americans rather than justice on their minds
- Viewable at: YouTube, Google Play, Apple TV, Vudu, Amazon Prime Video

Get Out

- First Black screenwriter to win an Oscar (Jordan Peele for Best Original Screenplay)
- A young African American visits his white girlfriend's parents for the weekend, where his simmering uneasiness about their reception of him eventually reaches a boiling point
- Viewable at: YouTube, Google Play, Apple TV, Vudu, Amazon Prime Video

Kings

- The life of a foster family in South Central Los Angeles, a few weeks before the city erupts in violence following the verdict of the Rodney King trial
- Viewable at: Starz, YouTube

Marshall

- The story of Thurgood Marshall, the crusading lawyer who would become the first African American Supreme Court Justice, as he battles through one of his career-defining cases
- Viewable at: YouTube, Google, Apple TV, Vudu, Amazon Prime Video

Mudbound

- Two men return home from World War II to work on a farm in rural Mississippi, where they struggle to deal with racism and adjusting to life after war
- Viewable at: Netflix

The Forgiven

- After the end of Apartheid, Archbishop Desmond Tutu meets with a brutal murderer seeking redemption
- Viewable at: YouTube, Amazon Prime Video

2018

BlacKkKlansman
- True story of Ron Stallworth, an African American police officer from Colorado Springs, CO, who successfully manages to infiltrate the local Ku Klux Klan branch with the help of a Jewish surrogate who eventually becomes its leader
- Viewable at: YouTube, Google Play, Apple TV, Vudu, Amazon Prime Video

Black Panther
- First Black Marvel superhero film to ever be released
- T'Challa, heir to the hidden but advanced kingdom of Wakanda, must step forward to lead his people into a new future and must confront a challenger from his country's past
- Huge box office hit and received multiple industry awards
- Viewable at: Disney+, TBS, TNT, Amazon Prime Video

Burden
- When a museum celebrating the Ku Klux Klan opens in a South Carolina town, the idealistic Reverend Kennedy strives to keep the peace even as he urges the group's Grand Dragon to disavow his racist past
- Viewable at: YouTube, Showtime

Canal Street
- After being arrested for the murder of a white classmate, a young Black man's father fights in court for his son's vindication
- Viewable at: Amazon Prime Video

Green Book
- A working-class Italian-American bouncer becomes the driver of a gay African American classical pianist on a tour of venues through the 1960s American South
- Won Best Picture Academy Award
- Viewable at: YouTube, Google Play, Apple TV, Vudu, Amazon Prime Video

If Beale Street Could Talk
- A young Black woman embraces her pregnancy while she and her family set out to prove her childhood friend and lover innocent of a crime he didn't commit
- Viewable at: YouTube, Google Play, Apple TV, Vudu, Amazon Prime Video

King In The Wilderness
- A look at the final years in the life of Martin Luther King, Jr.
- Viewable at: HBO Max, YouTube

The Hate U Give

- Starr witnesses the fatal shooting of her childhood best friend Khalil at the hands of a police officer. Now, facing pressure from all sides of the community, Starr must find her voice and stand up for what's right.
- Viewable at: YouTube, Google Play, Apple TV, Vudu, Amazon Prime Video

2019

American Son

- An estranged interracial couple reunite in a Florida police station to help find their missing teenage son who was in a car stopped by the police. Is he alive or dead and was his involvement with the other occupants of the car a result of his inability to fit into the white world he was raised in before his parents split?
- Viewable at: Netflix

The Best of Enemies

- Civil rights activist Ann Atwater faces off against C.P. Ellis, Exalted Cyclops of the Ku Klux Klan, in 1971 Durham, North Carolina over the issue of school integration
- Viewable at: Showtime, YouTube

Harriet

- The extraordinary tale of Harriet Tubman's escape from slavery and transformation into one of America's greatest heroes, whose courage, ingenuity, and tenacity freed hundreds of slaves and changed the course of history
- Viewable at:

Jojo Rabbit

- A young boy in Hitler's army finds out his mother is hiding a Jewish girl in their home
- Viewable at: Hulu, Amazon Prime Video, YouTube

Just Mercy

- World-renowned civil rights defense attorney Bryan Stevenson works to free a wrongly condemned death row prisoner
- Viewable at: Hulu, Amazon Prime Video, YouTube

2020

The Banker

- In the 1960s two African American entrepreneurs hire a working-class white man to pretend to be the head of their business empire while they pose as a janitor and chauffeur
- Viewable at: Apple TV

Foreign Films

The Eternal Jew (UK, 1934)

Triumph of the Will (Germany, 1935)

Circus (USSR, 1936)

The Eternal Jew (Germany, 1940)

Jud Süß (Germany, 1940)

Cry, the Beloved Country (UK, 1951)

Black Orpheus (Brazil, 1959)

Kiku to Isamu (Japan, 1959)

Flame in the Streets (UK, 1961)

Death By Hanging (Japan, 1968)

Pink Floyd – The Wall (UK, 1982)

Cry Freedom (UK, 1987)

For Queen and Country (UK, 1988)

Once Upon a Time in China (HK, 1992)

Romper Stomper (Australia, 1992)

Speak Up! It's So Dark (Sweden, 1993)

30:e november (Sweden, 1995)

Taxi (Spain, 1996)

La vita è bella (Italy, 1997)

Nattbuss 807 (Sweden, 1997)

East Is East (UK, 1999)

Saroja (Sri Lanka, 2000)

Khaled (Canada, 2001)

Little Angel (Sri Lanka, 2002)

Rabbit-Proof Fence (Australia, 2002)

Continuous Journey (Canada, 2004)

Amazing Grace (UK, 2006)

Brocket 99 - Rockin' the Country (Canada, 2006)

Steel Toes (Canada, 2006)

This Is England (UK, 2007)

Unrepentant: Kevin Annett and Canada's Genocide (Canada, 2007)

Skin (Africa, 2008)

Cedar Boys (Australia, 2009)

The Combination (Australia, 2009)

Toussaint Louverture (France, 2012)

Belle (UK, 2013)

Utopia (Australia, 2013)

A United Kingdom (UK, 2016)

Pariyerum Perumal (India, 2018)

Slam (Australia, 2018)

The Last Victims (South Africa, 2019)

Bibliography

Atkinson, J. Brooks. "Show Boat." *New York Times*. 28 December 1927

Atkinson, J. Brooks. "THE PLAY; Show Boat" as Good as New." *New York Times*. 20 May 1932.

Boroff, Philip. "'A Strange Loop' Expands Boundaries: Review," *Broadway Journal*, 18 June 2019, last accessed 13 October 2020, <http://broadwayjournal.com/navel-gazy-strange-loop-expands-boundaries-review/>.

Brantley, Ben. "Theater Review; 'Ragtime': A Diorama With Nostalgia Rampant," *The New York Times*, 19 January 1998, last accessed 3 November 2020, <https://www.nytimes.com/1998/01/19/theater/theater-review-ragtime-a-diorama-with-nostalgia-rampant.html>.

Brantley, Ben. "'The Color Purple' on Broadway, Stripped to Its Essence," The New York Times, 10 December 2015, last accessed 9 February 2021, <https://www.nytimes.com/2015/12/11/theater/review-the-color-purple-on-broadway-stripped-to-its-essence.html>.

Brantley, Ben. "Through Hot Pink Glasses, a World That's Nice," *The New York Times*, 16 August 2002, last accessed 14 December 2020, <https://www.nytimes.com/2002/08/16/movies/theater-review-through-hot-pink-glasses-a-world-that-s-nice.html>.

Chapman, John. "West Side Story, a Splendid and Super-Modern Musical Drama," *New York Daily News*, 27 September 1957, last accessed 18 December 2020, <https://www.nydailynews.com/entertainment/theater-arts/west-side-story-recounts-romeo-juliet-1957-article-1.2368364>.

Christiansen, Richard. "A Great Show When it Premiered, 'Ragtime' Gets Even Better in Chicago," *Chicago Tribune*, 9 November 1998, last accessed 3 November 2020 <https://www.chicagotribune.com/news/ct-xpm-1998-11-09-9811090026-story.html>.

Delmont, M. "'Hairspray' Is a Revealing Portrayal of Racism in America," *The Atlantic*. 23 November 2017, last accessed 6 December 2020, <https://www.theatlantic.com/entertainment/archive/2016/12/hairsprays-revealing-portrayal-of-racism-in-america/509741/>.

DiGiacomo, Frank. "'Hamilton's' Lin-Manuel Miranda on Finding Originality, Racial Politics (and Why Trump Should See His Show)." *The Hollywood Reporter*, 12 August 2015, last accessed 23 October 2020, <https://www.hollywoodreporter.com/features/hamiltons-lin-manuel-miranda-finding-814657>.

Evans, Greg. "*Ragtime*," *Variety*, 17 January 1998, last accessed 23 January 2021, <https://variety.com/1998/legit/reviews/ragtime-3-1117436764/>.

Gardner, Elysa. "A Strange Loop: The Cycle of Life, On Repeat," *New York Stage Review*, 17 June 2019, last accessed 13 October 2020, <http://nystagereview.com/2019/06/17/a-strange-loop-the-cycle-of-life-on-repeat/>.

Gerard, Jeremy. "Show Boat," *Variety*, 4 October 1994, last accessed 19 October 2020, <https://variety.com/1994/legit/reviews/show-boat-4-1200439114/>.

Kennedy, Gerrick D. "On its 40th anniversary, a look at how 'The Wiz' forever changed black culture," *Los Angeles Times*, 24 October 2018, last accessed 9 February 2021, <https://www.latimes.com/entertainment/music/la-et-ms-the-wiz-40-anniversary-20181024-story.html>.

Krasner, David. "A Beautiful Pageant: African American Theatre," *Drama and Performance in the Harlem Renaissance*, 1910-1927, Palgrave MacMillan, 2002, pp. 263–67.

Lee, Jasen. "'Once on This Island' discusses issues of race and class in communities of color," *Deseret News*, 21 February 2020, last accessed 17 November 2020, <https://www.deseret.com/utah/2020/2/21/21144374/once-on-this-island-utah-race-colorism-class-love-pioneer-theater>.

Mead, Rebecca. "All About the Hamiltons," *The New Yorker*, 9 February 2015, last accessed 17 November 2020, <https://www.newyorker.com/magazine/2015/02/09/hamiltons>.

Paulsen, M. (July 12, 2015). "'Hamilton' Heads to Broadway in a Hip-Hop Retelling" Archived October 1, 2015, at the Wayback Machine. *The New York Times*. Retrieved August 17, 2015.

Peterson, Russel. "I Was a Teenage Negro! Blackface as a Vehicle of White Liberalism in Finian's Rainbow," *American Studies*, Vol. 47, No. 3/4, last accessed 9 February 2021, <https://www.jstor.org/stable/40643953?seq=1#metadata_info_tab_contents>.

Pollack-Pelzner, Daniel. "Why West Side Story Abandoned Its Queer Narrative," *The Atlantic*, 1 March 2020, last accessed 18 December 2020, <https://www.theatlantic.com/culture/archive/2020/03/ivo-van-hoves-west-side-story-steeped-stereotypes/607210/>.

Rich, Frank. "'Once on This Island,' Fairy Tale Bringing Caribbean to 42nd Street," *The New York Times*, 7 May 1990, last accessed 17 November 2020, <https://www.nytimes.com/1990/05/07/theater/review-theater-once-on-this-island-fairy-tale-bringing-caribbean-to-42d-street.html>.

Rizzo, Frank. "Off Broadway Review: 'A Strange Loop,'" *Variety*, 17 June 2019, last accessed 13 October 2020, <https://variety.com/2019/legit/reviews/a-strange-loop-review-musical-1203245457/>.

Soloski, Alexis. "'The violence should be tangible' – Ivo van Hove on roughing up West Side Story," *The Guardian*, 17 February 2020, last accessed 18 December 2020, <https://www.theguardian.com/stage/2020/feb/17/west-side-story-broadway-new-york-ivo-van-hove-anne-teresa-de-keersmaeker-violence>.

Teachout, Terry. "Shuffle Along Review: Half of Perfection", *The Wall Street Journal*, April 28, 2016.

Woll, Allen. *Black Musicals: From Coontown to Dreamgirls* (1989), Da Capo Press, p. 78.

A Brief Biography of Professor Walter Palmer

After a tumultuous juvenile life, Professor Palmer graduated from high school and was hired by the University of Pennsylvania hospital as a surgical attendant and eventually was recruited into the University of Pennsylvania School of Inhalation and Respiratory (Oxygen) Therapy.

After his certification as an inhalation and respiratory therapist, he was hired by the Children's Hospital of Philadelphia as the Director of the Department of Inhalation and Respiratory (Oxygen) Therapy, where he spent ten years helping to develop the national field of cardio-pulmonary therapy.

In 1955, Professor Palmer created the Palmer Foundation and the Black People's University of Philadelphia Freedom School and would spend the next seventy years developing leaders for social justice nationally.

Professor Palmer has also pursued further education at Temple University for Business Administration and Communications, Cheyney State University for a Teacher's Degree in History and Secondary Education. And at age 40, acquired his juris doctorate in law from Howard University.

Between 1965 and 1995, he produced and hosted radio programs on Philadelphia WDAS, Atlantic City WUSS, and WFPG Radio, in addition to Philadelphia NBC TV 10 and New Jersey Suburban Cable Television.

In 2006, he was inducted into the Philadelphia College of Physicians as a Fellow for the body of work he had done over the past 70 years, after having spent ten (1980-1990) years as a licensed financial officer teaching poor people how to overcome poverty by saving and investing three dollars per day.

During that entire period, Professor Palmer led the Civil Rights, Black Power and Afrocentric movements in Philadelphia, around the country as well as the Caribbean and West Indies.

In the 1980s to 2015, he led the school choice movement, organized a state-wide parental school choice group which collected 500,000 petitions in 1997, which were used to create a charter and cyber school law in Pennsylvania, and in 2000 the Walter D. Palmer School was named after him.

In 1962, he created a school without walls on the University of Pennsylvania's campus and became a visiting lecturer in the Schools of Medicine, Law, Education, Wharton, History, Africana Studies, Engineering, and he currently is a lecturer in the Schools of Medicine, Social Work, and Urban Studies, where he teaches courses on American racism.

In 1969, he helped the University of Pennsylvania Graduate School of Social Work students and faculty create required courses on American racism, making the University of Pennsylvania the first school in American academia to have such courses.

In 2019, Professor Palmer was appointed to the President's Commission on commemorating the four hundred year (1619) anniversary of American slavery.

Over his many years of teaching, he has received the title of Teacher Par Excellence and has amassed over 1,000 medals, trophies, plaques, certificates, and awards for participation in multiple disciplines.

W.D. Palmer Foundation Publications

The Palmer Foundation was founded in 1955 and is a 501(c)3 tax-exempt organization that has spent over 65 years developing educational curriculum and learning materials for at-risk children, their parents, mentors, and teachers across the country.

We work with children from pre-school to high school with a focus on leadership, self-development, and social awareness.

Community Survivalist

Community Activist

International Activist

Human Rights Advocate

Contact Us
The W.D. Palmer Foundation (1955)
P.O. Box 22692
Philadelphia, PA 19110
(267) 738-1588
thewdpalmerfoundation@gmail.com
www.thewdpalmerfoundation.org
www.speakerservices.com

Donate to the W.D. Palmer Foundation

Make a donation (purchase), from the W.D. Palmer Foundation, a 501(c)3 tax-exempt organization that has worked for over 65 years to educate urban and rural "at-risk" children and their families, since 1955.

We have developed and published education curriculum and learning materials on leadership, self-development, and social awareness and how to overcome illiteracy, poverty, crime, and racism for urban and rural at-risk children and their families.

You will get a bulk discount for fifty (50) books or more, and the larger the order, the greater the discount. If you need less than fifty books, please order them directly from the publisher using the information below.

Order from us:
The W.D. Palmer Foundation
P.O. Box 22692
Philadelphia, PA 19110
www.thewdpalmerfoundation.org
wdpalmer@gmail.com
(267) 738-1588

Order from our publisher:
Author House
1663 Liberty Drive
Bloomington, IN 47403
www.authorhouse.com
(833) 262-8899

Part-time income
The W.D. Palmer Foundation is looking for community members and students that would like to earn extra income as independent sales representatives. Contact us to learn more.

Race and Racism

All Ebooks are $3.99+

Racism in American Stage and Screen

How American stage and movies fostered racism in America and around the world.

Racism in America and Black Mental Health

How Black people were affected mentally by race and racism in America.

The W.D. Palmer Foundation

thewdpalmerfoundation@gmail.com thewdpalmerfoundation.org

History

All Ebooks are $3.99+

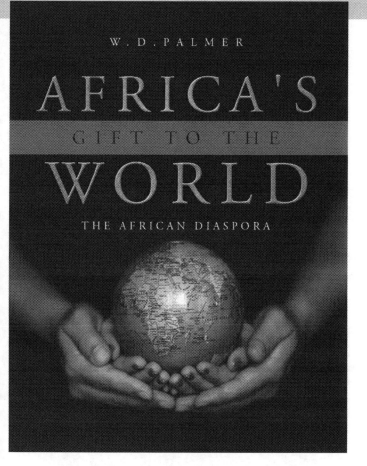

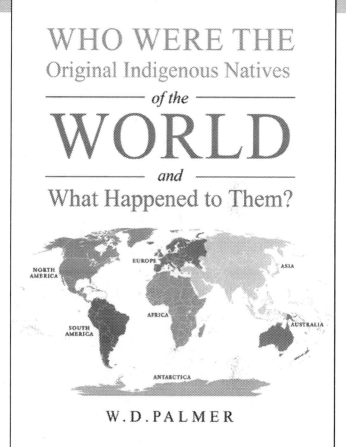

Africa's Gift to the World: The African Diaspora

How African humanity, culture, civilization, and history were spread all over the world through slavery.

Who were the Original Indigenous Natives of the World?

An attempt to answer questions of where people came from and where they went.

The W.D. Palmer Foundation
thewdpalmerfoundation@gmail.com thewdpalmerfoundation.org

Race, Racism, and Entertainment

All Ebooks are $3.99+

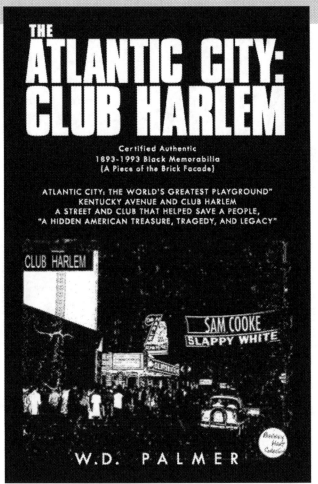

The Atlantic City Club Harlem

The story of how a nightclub was used to break down race and racism barriers in a small town.

MADD About Freedom

Major contributors in Music, Art, Dance, and Drama who used their talents for freedom.

The W.D. Palmer Foundation
thewdpalmerfoundation@gmail.com   thewdpalmerfoundation.org

Leadership

All Ebooks are $3.99+

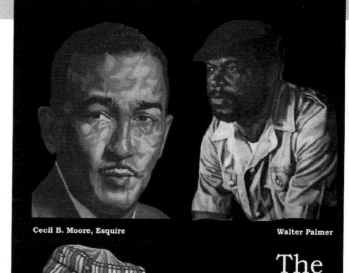

From David Walker to Jesse Jackson

Some of the most vocal people who spoke out for freedom.

Philadelphia Civil Rights Activists: 1950-2000

How two men helped shape the history and destiny of a major metropolitan city.

The W.D. Palmer Foundation

thewdpalmerfoundation@gmail.com thewdpalmerfoundation.org

Youth Advocacy

All Ebooks are $3.99+

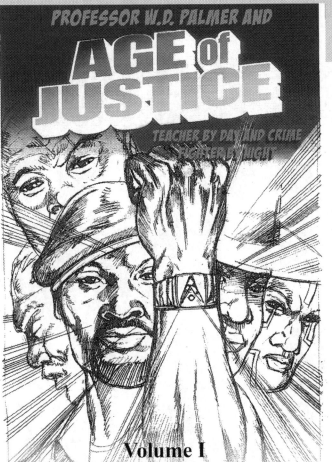

Volume I

Appeal to all elementary, middle, high school, and college students
and their parents to join the fight for social change!

Adopt an elementary, middle, high school, or college student, class,
or school, or a church, for them to receive this survival guide

Volume I:
Alcohol Abuse
Animal Abuse
Asbestos
Bullying
Child Abuse
Disability
Disability Discrimination
Domestic Abuse
Drug Abuse
Education Discrimination

Volume II:
Elder Abuse
Employment Discrimination
Environmental Abuse
Ethnic Discrimination
Fighting
Fire Safety
Gambling Abuse
Gangs
Gender Discrimination
COVID-19

Volume III:
Gun Violence
Hate Crimes
HIV/AIDS
Homelessness
Housing Discrimination
Human Trafficking
Hunger
Labor Trafficking
Lead Poisoning
LGBT Discrimination

Volume IV:
Mental Health
Nutrition
Obesity
Pedophilia
Poison
Police Abuse
Public Accom. Discrim.
Racial Discrimination
Religious Discrimination
Runaways

Volume V:
School Dropout
Sex Trafficking
Sexual Assault
Sexual Harassment
Special Education
STDS
Stealing
Suicide
Teen Pregnancy
Water Safety

Professor W.D. Palmer and Age of Justice

A real-life comic hero appeal to parents, teachers, ministers, coaches, mentors, and monitors on how to help elementary, middle, high school, and first-year college students on where to turn in the face of danger.

The W.D. Palmer Foundation
thewdpalmerfoundation@gmail.com thewdpalmerfoundation.org

World Leaders

All Ebooks are $3.99+

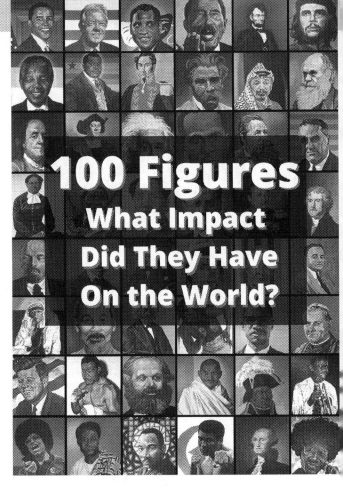

From Civil Rights Activists to Human Rights Advocates

How the fight for civil rights transformed activists into human rights advocates.

100 Figures

In what ways did 100 individuals impact the world?

The W.D. Palmer Foundation

thewdpalmerfoundation@gmail.com   thewdpalmerfoundation.org

W. D. Palmer Foundation Hashtags

1. #racedialogueusa
2. #racismdialogueusa
3. #atriskchildrenusa
4. #youthorganizingusa
5. #stopblackonblackusa
6. #newleadershipusa
7. #1619commemorationusa
8. #africanslaveryusa
9. #indigenouspeopleusa
10. #afrocentricusa
11. #civillibertiesusa
12. #civilrightsusa
13. #humanrightsusa
14. #saveourchildrenusa
15. #parentalschoolchoiceusa
16. #wearyourmaskusa
17. #defeatcovid19usa
18. #socialdistanceusa

Printed in the United States
by Baker & Taylor Publisher Services